TOOLS
AND
TENANTS

TOONS AND TENANTS

Settlement and society in Shetland, 1299-1899

Brian Smith

The Shetland Times Ltd.,
Lerwick
2000

Toons and Tenants
Copyright © Brian Smith, 2000

ISBN 1-898852-68-5

First published by The Shetland Times Ltd, 2000
Reprinted 2003

Cover photographs:
Background: The communal meadows of North Cunningsburgh on an August day in the 1920s. *Copyright Shetland Museum.*
Bottom insert : The Sandison family unload peats at the home peat stack of Rögert, Muness, Unst, around 1904 (photograph by Tom Kent). They have 'flit' the peats by pony from the Ness of Muness; now they unload them and begin to build the stack. *Copyright Shetland Museum.*

All rights reserved
No part of this publication may be reproduced, stored in a retrieval system or transmitted, in any form, by any means, electronic, mechanical, photocopying, recording or otherwise, without the prior written permission of the publishers.

British Library Cataloguing-in-Publication Data.
A catalogue record for this book is available from the British Library.

Printed and published by
The Shetland Times Ltd,
Gremista,
Lerwick, Shetland, ZE1 0PX, UK.

For my mother
and in memory of my father

CONTENTS

Introduction xi
    Outline of chronology xv
    Shetland's coinless currency, 1300-1700 xvi
1. The letter of 1299 about Papa Stour 1
    A note on sources and anomalies 16
2. Lasts of land 19
    A note on toonmels 32
3. What is a scattald? 37
    A note on waithing and waith 58
4. Rents from the sea 65
Appendix: Documents 81
Index 98

FIGURES

1. Map of Shetland, with places mentioned in the text. xvii
2. Bragister, Papa Stour. 2
3. Papa Stour in c.1650. 12
4. Papa Stour in c.1299. 13
5. Harrowing at Udhoose, Delting. 20
6. Culswick, Sandsting. 23
7. The meadows of North Cunningsburgh. 27
8. Funzie, Fetlar. 30
9. Toonmels at Collaquey, Northmavine. 33
10. Leveneep, Lunnasting. 34
11. Da Forrats, Sandness. 34
12. Toons at Wester Quarff. 35
13. Grunnavoe, Waas. 35
14. The hill dyke at Benigert, Nort Roe. 38
15. Cattle on hill pasture. 41
16. Closing the hill grind. 43
17. John Walker and Mary Plummer. 49
18. Croft clearances and scattald confiscations in Shetland, c.1820-c.1875. 50-1
19. Gert, Dunrossness, c.1870. 53
20. Gert, Dunrossness, c.1880. 53
21. The waithing skerries of Burrafirth. 57
22. Whales at Sand, 1899. 63
23. Symbister, c.1904. 66
24. The bød and beach at Hillswick, c.1880. 69
25. A sixern sets off to the haaf from Fedeland, c.1890. 74
26. A steeple of fish. 77

Introduction

In 1883 Charles Rampini described a 'Shetland "town"', for the benefit of Lord Napier's crofting commission.[1] It was, he said,

> [a] collection of cottages built of stone and generally straw-thatched, surrounded by feul dykes, which separate the township from its hill-pasture or scattald. In front of the cottages are the town-maills—a piece of ground always left uncultivated, and on which are tethered the stock required by the crofters for their domestic use. Lower down are the kail-yards of the cottagers, and patches of arable growing crops of bere, potatoes or oats, always unfenced, and sometimes held in runrig.

The essays in this little book are about the 700 or so 'toons' where medieval and modern Shetlanders lived. They are also about the way that the Shetlanders divided and assessed their lands, and about the rent that tenants paid to landlords, from the thirteenth to the nineteenth centuries. Throughout I try to relate technical details to change in the relations of production, and to the rise and fall of classes.

*

Some writers about these subjects have been imaginative. Captain F.W.L. Thomas suggested in 1884 that King Harald Fairhair of Norway (fl. 900) valued the townships of Shetland, Orkney and the Western Isles in 'pennylands' and 'ouncelands', so that he could collect pennies and ounces of tax from them.[2] Fifty years later Hugh Marwick announced that these pennylands and ouncelands became assessment units for furnishing the Orkney earls' war-fleets.[3]

In these scenarios the townships are significant only insofar as they provide revenue and manpower for kings and earls. The Marwick-Thomas theses have been popular, but they are unconvincing. As we shall see, they depend on the existence of a mark of the ninth- or tenth-century divided into 144 pennies.[4] There was no such mark. Secondly, there is no reason to conclude that a pennyland paid a penny of tax, any more than a markland paid a mark of tax.[5] But that was Thomas's

---

1. *Parliamentary Papers* 1884, xxxiii, minutes of evidence, p.1403. 'Feul' is of course 'feal': Rampini's handwriting was execrable.
2. F.W.L. Thomas, 'What is a pennyland? or ancient valuation of land in the Scottish Isles', *Proceedings of the Society of Antiquaries of Scotland*, vi, 1883-4, pp.258, 284.
3. Hugh Marwick, 'Leidang in the west', *Proceedings of the Orkney Antiquarian Society*, xiii, 1934-5, pp.15-29.
4. Thomas and Marwick claimed that the Orkney and Shetland mark was divided into sterling pennies, at some unspecified but very early period (Thomas, 'What is a pennyland', p.258; Marwick, 'Leidang in the west', p.21). Per Sveaas Andersen follows them, albeit with a different chronology ('When was regular, annual taxation introduced in the Norse islands of Britain? a comparative study of assessment systems in north-western Europe', *Scandinavian Journal of History*, xvi, 1991, p.81). True, in the 1320s-1330s in Bergen a burnt mark was worth 12 English shillings (Asgaut Steinnes, 'Mynt-rekning på 13-hundradtalet', *Historisk Tidsskrift* [Norwegian], 5th series, vii, 1927-9, p.392). But the proposition that there was a similar exchange-rate in the ninth or tenth century (Thomas and Marwick), or the twelfth (Andersen), is outrageous. As we shall see (p.6, *infra*), sterling isn't the only currency in the world.
5. W.F. Skene had actually made the suggestion before Thomas: *John of Fordun's Chronicle of the Scottish Nation*, ii, Edinburgh 1872, p.450.

most successful proposition: even those who reject his chronology have accepted it without question. Thirdly, Thomas and Marwick accepted without qualm that tax was levied on *land* in Orkney and Shetland of the tenth century. It is far more likely that taxes of that period were exacted from *individuals*, as in Norway.[6] I propose that the pennylands and ouncelands had nothing to do with tax, in their original incarnation, and everything to do with the division of arable land into 18 shares: their main function at all times. Fourthly, it is naïve to assume that institutions with the same name in widely separate places had the same origin. Otherwise we might conclude that the ouncelands of South Wales[7] and the pennylands of Gloucestershire[8] were also Harald's work. There is no likelihood, I suggest, and certainly no proof, that the 18-pennyland 'ureslands' of the Northern Isles and the 20-pennyland 'unciates' and 'tirungas' of the Western Isles were related. Certainly their names are different. Finally, is there evidence that Orkney and Shetland had a sophisticated levy-system in saga-time? No. Marwick's reconstruction is based on alleged resemblances – in my view fanciful – between tax-payments in Orkney in the sixteenth century and Norwegian payments of the same period.[9]

Thomas and his followers were enthralled by the alleged *origins* of institutions, and little else.

*

I am interested in the fiscal material that Thomas and Marwick tried to expound, but I proceed in a different direction. I argue (Chapter 1) that Shetland's pennylands date from (at the earliest) the late eleventh century, and that her characteristic land-rents and land-taxes emerged even later. These are not antiquarian matters: as we shall see, land-rent was central in the Shetland and Norwegian polities of the high and late middle ages.[10] Medieval Shetland, like Norway, was a land of tenants.

Secondly, I focus on the internal arrangements of our toons (Chapter 2). I bring to the forefront Shetland's 'lasts of land' and their constituent 'marks of land': tools to create *shares* of arable. Here we must deal with problems of runrig, so characteristic of Shetland's toons in the nineteenth and even the twentieth centuries.[11]

Thirdly, I trace the political economy of Shetland's rural communities over a long period: from the high middle ages to the brink of the twentieth century (Chapters 3

---

6. Halvard Bjørkvik, 'Nefgildi', in *Kulturhistorisk Leksikon for Nordisk Middelalder*, xii, Copenhagen 1981, cols. 279-81.
7. Wendy Davies, *'Unciae:* land measurement in the *Liber Landavensis'*, *Agricultural History Review,* xxi, 1973, pp.111-2.
8. William Henry Hart ed., *Historia et Cartularium Monasterii Sancti Petri Gloucestræ*, iii, London 1867, pp. xvii, 123.
9. D.G.E. Williams, 'Land assessment and military organisation in the Norse settlements in Scotland, c.900-1266 AD', unpublished university of St Andrews Ph.D., 1996, comprehensively disposes of Marwick's argument.
10. Marwick didn't grasp this point. His treatment of land-rent, as opposed to taxation, is cursory: 'Rents are so familiar a feature of life still today that they call for no further notice' (Hugh Marwick, *Orkney Farm-Names,* Kirkwall 1952, p.205).
11. Otherwise I pay virtually no attention to methods of agriculture in the islands. For an exemplary account of such matters, in a different but comparable geographical setting, see Robert Dodgshon, *From Chiefs to Landlords: social and economic change in the Western Highlands and Islands, c.1493-1820,* Edinburgh 1998.

and 4). Marwick & Co. thought that Orkney, and presumably Shetland, ceased to have a history after 1600.[12] However, most of our records of the islands' traditional rural institutions date from the sixteenth and seventeenth centuries, and we have to look at that era – an age of equipoise in the islands – with special care. Thus I describe the fortunes of Shetland's 'scattalds' (Chapter 3), which remained unenclosed, and provided nurture for all their inhabitants, for hundreds of years. Shetland remained a 'peasant-based' society for a long time.[13]

I go on to show how Shetland's economic history changed course during the eighteenth and nineteenth centuries (Chapters 3 and 4), and how the structure of settlement and relations of production in the islands altered as a result. In these chapters I am at pains to discover the nature of the peasant bondage and 'fishing tenure' that flourished here until the late nineteenth century.

I began to look at these matters in 1967, and redoubled my attempts to understand them in 1987. Why study the rural communities of a poor country like Shetland? I ask because metropolitan historians sometimes regard regional studies with disdain, unlike their colleagues in other disciplines. As Raphael Samuel put it:[14]

> In archaeology [the region's] relics are given equal weight to those of England in reconstituting patterns of religion or settlement. Sociologists, discussing 'communities in Britain', will refer as easily to family and community in Co. Clare – or villages on the Welsh border – as to family and kinship in East London. ... Matters are quite different for the student, or teacher, of British history...

It is important for Shetlanders to understand their history; but I hope that history can be instructive to others as well. It isn't self-evident that the decline of heritable jurisdictions in Scotland or Shetland is less important than the secularization of the parish in Buckinghamshire, or that carucates are more momentous than lasts of land.

There is another uneasy relationship between centre and periphery. Until recently Norwegian historians paid little attention to the islands' history. There is a mere handful of references to Shetland in the indispensable *Kulturhistorisk Leksikon for Nordisk Middelalder*, and Sigvald Hasund and Andreas Holmsen, great historians of medieval Norway, only devoted a couple of sentences to us. At the same time, most Shetlanders couldn't read the work of the Norwegian agrarian school, and didn't try. During the 1990s historians like Steinar Imsen turned their attention to the islands in the west.[15] I hope that this little book returns the compliment.

*

There are four main essays in the volume, written at intervals over the past 16 years and now revised to a greater or lesser extent.

---

12. Hugh Marwick, *Orkney*, London 1951, p.99: 'From the time of the Stewart earls the history of Orkney is mainly economic, and will be touched on in a later chapter.' Touched on!
13. I borrow this phrase from Chris Wickham, *Land and Power: studies in Italian and European social history 400-1200*, London 1994, pp.217, 224-5. Wickham is writing about a much earlier period, but his epithet is applicable to Shetland of the sixteenth and seventeenth centuries.
14. Raphael Samuel, 'In search of Britain', *New Statesman and Society*, 25 August 1989, pp.21-2.
15. Steinar Imsen, *Norske Bondekommunalisme fra Magnus Lagabøte til Kristian Kvart, 1: Middelalderen*, Trondheim 1990; *Norske Bondekommunalisme fra Magnus Lagabøte til Kristian Kvart 2: Lydriketiden*, Trondheim 1994.

'The letter of 1299 about Papa Stour' is a version of a paper I gave at the Papa Stour conference in Lerwick in July 1999.

I delivered the paper 'Lasts of land' to a meeting of the Society of Northern Studies in Edinburgh in November 1999. It is followed by a note on 'toonmels' which appeared in Hugh Cheape ed., *Tools and Tradition*, Edinburgh 1993.

I first wrote 'What is a scattald' for a *heiðursrit* to honour my friend the late Dr T.M.Y. Manson: *Essays in Shetland History*, edited by Barbara Crawford (Lerwick 1984). It is followed here by a note on 'waithing' which appeared in the *Shetland Folk Book*, vol. ix, in 1995.

The final paper first saw the light of day at a joint seminar of the Scottish History Department and Scottish Institute of Maritime Studies in St Andrews University, in November 1989. It was published in *Scotland and the Sea*, edited by T.C. Smout (Edinburgh 1992).

Public and other records held by the National Archives of Scotland are quoted with the approval of the Keeper of the Records of Scotland.

I am indebted to Tommy Watt for permission to publish photographs from the Shetland Museum's fine collection. Bob Crawford supplied the photograph of Bragister, taken on the halcyon day when sixty conference delegates visited Papa Stour in July 1999. These photographs illustrate the shape of Shetland townships, and the agricultural and fishing activities that Shetlanders engaged in until a relatively recent date.

I am very grateful to Willie Thomson, who has been discussing these questions with me for more years than we care to recall. He has kindly read the whole text, and made stimulating suggestions. John Ballantyne has shared his archival discoveries with me, and pursued references for me, over an almost equally long period. He too read the manuscript with eagle eye. Michael Barnes, Paul Bibire, Barbara Crawford, Knut Helle, Steinar Imsen, Tom Schmidt and Gareth Williams have been extremely helpful to me over the years.

For information about specific subjects I am indebted to Per Sveaas Andersen, Malcolm Bangor-Jones, Bruce Benson, Wilma Cluness, Susan Cooper, John Coutts, Peter Foote, the late Alan Fraser, Christie Fraser, Mary Fraser, Peder Gammeltoft, the late George Gear, Wendy Gear, Jo Hanlon, Lars Ivar Hansen, the late Tom Henderson, the late Freda Hutchison, John Jamieson, Robbie Jarmson, John Jeromson, Robert Leask, Lindsay Macgregor, Keetie Malcolmson, Jane Manson, Bertie Mathewson, Stewart Moore, Alfhild Nakken, Pamela Nightingale, Ingvild Øye, Jennifer Perry, George P.S. Peterson, Jóhan Hendrik W. Poulsen, David Rhind, Jørn Sandnes, Ann Sinclair, Cissie Smith, Þorsteinn Vilhjálmsson, the late Tom Tulloch, Aggie Walterson, Gordon Walterson and Harald Witthöft.

Gordon Johnston advised me on stylistic matters; Ian Tait helped me choose illustrations, and devise informative captions for them; Vicki Gowans printed photos. Ballantyne, Johnston, Tait and other friends have accompanied me on outings, in slester and sunshine, to some of the toons I discuss.

Brian Smith
23 April 2000

Outline of chronology

Circa late eleventh – early twelfth centuries Adoption of Cologne mark of 12 shillings in Shetland and Orkney? Assessment of Shetland and Orkney townships in 'ouncelands' (or fractions of ouncelands) and 'pennylands' (18 per ounceland).
Twelfth century Reassessment of Shetland and Orkney pennylands in 'marks of land'.
1195 Shetland confiscated by King Sverre from the earl of Orkney. Shetland's rural institutions begin to diverge from those of Orkney.
Easter 1299 Ragnhild Simunsdatter's dispute with Thorvald Thoresson, about the fiscal status of the marginal township of Bragister in the island of Papa Stour. A revaluation of land, building on the old assessment systems, seems to have taken place during the administration of Duke Håkon Magnusson. Shetland's characteristic rent- and tax-systems may date from this period.
1349 The Black Death arrives in Shetland.
Late middle ages Shetland's ouncelands and pennylands go out of use, and are eventually replaced by similar units called 'lasts' and 'half lasts' of land, which comprise c.18 or c.9 marks of land, and pay 12 or 6 'shillings' of rent.
Early fifteenth century Merchants from North Germany begin to trade directly with Shetland.
1469 King of Denmark mortgages his rights in Shetland to the King of Scotland.
Sixteenth century – mid-seventeenth century Shetland townships now pay rent and tax in Shetland 'pennies' of cloth ('wadmal') and butter, rather than in corn as formerly. The population of the islands probably rises to around 12,000.
Late seventeenth century – early eighteenth century Crisis in the economy; disease; the German merchants stop coming to Shetland.
Eighteenth century Shetland's economy changes gear, following the crises; local 'merchant-lairds' take control. Fishing becomes a condition of tenure for most Shetlanders; in practice tenants now pay their rents in fish.
1747 Abolition of heritable jurisdictions and bailie courts.
Late eighteenth century – early nineteenth century Last vestiges of ancient system of rent-payment, and last instances of division of townships according to the last of land. During and after the Napoleonic wars commercial activity in the islands quickens and the economy diversifies. The population begins to rise rapidly, from about 20,000 in 1790 to about 26,000 in 1821.
1820 By now Shetland runrig exhibits extreme fragmentation and dispersal.
1820s - 1840s and 1860s - 1870s Two phases of clearance of Shetland townships and confiscation of scattalds. The population of the islands reaches its highest level – about 32,000 – between 1861 - 71, but falls by 2,000 by 1881, mainly due to the second phase of clearance.
1878 Beginning of a major herring fishery in the islands. Fishing tenure rapidly disappears.
1886 Shetland crofters acquire security of tenure, and in 1889 and 1892 they get fair rents.

Shetland's coinless currency, 1300-1700

In the high and late middle ages Norway was a country without large numbers of coins, and there can be little doubt that Shetland also had a dearth of them. Norwegians and Shetlanders therefore paid for goods, debts and fines with other goods. Local coinless currencies emerged, modelled on real coins and their subdivisions; medieval Norwegians and Shetlanders both 'define[d] an *eyrir* or a *mörk* as the *equivalent of a certain amount of goods*'.[16]

There is a revealing early reference to Shetland's currency. Some time before 1307 a woman called Biorg, a landowner in Yell, came to an agreement with Thorvald Thoresson, the king's representative in the islands. (For much more about Thorvald see Chapter 1, *infra*.) Biorg got the opportunity to redeem some land by paying *'iij merkr brendar j Hiatlenzkum æyre'*.[17] Kåre Lunden suggests that this means 'three marks burnt silver, paid in the kind of "money" usual in Shetland'.[18] According to Lunden the payment was probably meant to be made in cloth, but it might have been rendered in any kind of goods: Biorg in due course got permission to redeem her land with payment in butter: *'með smærgilldum æyre'*.

As we shall see (Chapter 1), Shetland's mark contained 12 'shillings' or 144 'pennies', and I suggest that it was modelled on the Cologne mark of the high middle ages. The last explicit reference to this Shetland mark is in a document of 1538, where a local court adjudged to a Shetlander '21 marks burnt in land, 12 Shetland shillings in every mark burnt, in Shetland wares'.[19]

Another local currency unit, also based on a German coin, emerged in the late middle ages: in 1465 someone paid six 'gylline' of linen cloth for a parcel of land.[20] This important unit appears in Shetland documents during subsequent centuries in such forms as 'gullioun' and 'gudling'.

Shetland pennies, shillings and gulliouns were still in common use in the late sixteenth and early seventeenth centuries, as 'Yetland payment'[21] for 'cuntrie wairis'.[22] There is even a reference to 'Yeitland payment' of pounds and shillings (£19 10s.) in a document of 1572.[23] In 1603 an official in the parish of Whiteness had to pay someone 'ane Yeitland schilling as for the price of ane yeir auld ox stirk put in fostering'.[24] A few years later the bed and board of Gutrom Lowrancesone

---

16. Kåre Lunden, 'Money economy in medieval Norway', *Scandinavian Journal of History*, xxiv, 1999, p.250. His italics.
17. *Diplomatarium Norvegicum*, i, no. 109.
18. Kåre Lunden, 'Money economy in medieval Norway', *Scandinavian Journal of History*, xxiv, 1999, p.255.
19. John H. Ballantyne and Brian Smith eds., *Shetland Documents 1195-1579*, Lerwick 1999, no. 59.
20. John H. Ballantyne and Brian Smith eds., *Shetland Documents 1195-1579*, Lerwick 1999, no. 24. For a similar development in Faroe see Louis Zachariasen, 'Hin føroyski gyllinin', in *Føroyar sum Rættarsamfelag*, Tórshavn 1961, pp.392ff.
21. John H. Ballantyne and Brian Smith eds., *Shetland Documents 1195-1579*, Lerwick 1999, nos. 139, 177, 211, appendix 4; John H. Ballantyne and Brian Smith eds., *Shetland Documents 1580-1611*, Lerwick 1994, nos. 19, 272, 351.
22. 'the auld lauchfull pryce of the barrell of drinking beir was and suld be for thre gudlingis of cuntrie wairis, sic as of fische, buttir, wadmell, or uther cuntrie wairis': John H. Ballantyne and Brian Smith eds., *Shetland Documents 1195-1579*, Lerwick 1999, p.198.
23. John H. Ballantyne and Brian Smith eds., *Shetland Documents 1195-1579*, Lerwick 1999, no. 193.
24. Gordon Donaldson ed., *The Court Book of Shetland 1602-1604*, Edinburgh 1954, p.103.

with his relatives was valued at 'ane Yetland d.' daily 'induring the spece of fayve yeiris' that he had lodged with them, 'extending for the said fayve yeiris to [150] gulliounis'.[25]

Even human beings could be valued in gulliouns. In 1612 the sheriff court of Shetland decided that it would be illegal for 'servile persons not worth thrie skoir gulyeonis, quhilk is lxxii li. Scottis, to take up houssis'.[26]

In the 1620s Shetlanders still paid rent and tax, and bought land, with pennies and gulliouns of goods. Tenants paid rent of four to 12 pennies per mark of land: a sixpenny mark, for instance, paid four pennies of cloth ('wadmal') + two pennies of butter; a ninepenny mark six pennies + three pennies. Most Shetlanders paid tax in the same way.[27] At the same date they were still paying a mark of goods for an average mark of land. In 1626 John Tulloch obliged himself to sell land to his brother in law[28]

> for the lyk and selfsame conditiounes and lands pryce as the lyk landis of rentaill within the contrey hes bein and is in use to be sauld for, according to the ald pryces of the said countrie of Yetland, viz. ... tuelf gulyeounes for the mark land sex d. the mark.

Shetland currency fell into disuse as the seventeenth century progressed, but the gullioun lingered on until the 1690s. Delinquents before the kirk session of Tingwall were still paying fines in 'gulones' between 1675-93.[29] In two contracts of 1695 between a Shetland landlord and some Dundee merchants there are references to stock fish measured in 'gullien' or 'double leispund called gullien leispund' of stock fish.[30] A century ago people in the isolated district of Yell called Da Herra still had faint memories of the word. By that time it had come to mean a hundredweight of fish, or, metaphorically, 'a trifle, a small weight of fish; a poor profit from fishing'.[31]

---

25. John H. Ballantyne and Brian Smith eds., *Shetland Documents 1195-1579*, Lerwick 1999, Appendix 6. Here a gulioun = more or less a Shetland shilling (365 x 5 ÷ 12). Cf. the statement in a document of 1589 that there were 'twelf goullovins to ilk mark' of 'lous gudis' (John H. Ballantyne and Brian Smith eds., *Shetland Documents 1580-1611*, Lerwick 1994, no. 159). Just as there had been 12 shillings in a Shetland mark, there came to be 12 gulliouns in a mark as well.
26. Robert S. Barclay ed., *The Court Book of Orkney and Shetland 1612-1613*, Kirkwall 1962, p.20.
27. See Appendix, p.84, *infra*.
28. See Appendix, p.82, *infra*.
29. Shetland Archives, CH.2/1078/1, folios 1, 5, 6, 7, 9, 26, 28, 30, 31, 33, 34, 35, 37: Kirk session register of Tingwall, 1675-1708.
30. Shetland Archives, SC.12/53/1, pp.46 and 52. 150 years previously '1 gylden in Hieltland' had likewise been 'equal to 2 "punds" of fish' (John H. Ballantyne and Brian Smith eds., *Shetland Documents 1195-1579*, Lerwick 1999, no. 91).
31. Jakob Jakobsen, *An Etymological Dictionary of the Norn Language in Shetland*, London 1928-32 ('gollen').

Figure 1 Map of Shetland showing places mentioned in the text.

1

The letter of 1299 about Papa Stour

> As a problem of history – perhaps the oldest problem of our history – it would be of great interest to ascertain when and by what authority, by what masters – political masters, or territorial – the western half of Scotland, the wildest shores of our Highlands, and the wildest islands, were measured and valued in marklands, shillinglands, pennylands, farthinglands, long before money – coined silver – was generally used or known as an element of rent, on the other side – the agricultural side of Scotland.
> - Cosmo Innes, *Lectures on Scotch Legal Antiquities*, Edinburgh 1872, p.275

Shetland's oldest document, a letter of 1299 about Papa Stour,[32] consists of just 360 words. Its *purpose* is clear. It's a public letter about an investigation, written down under the auspices of officials in Shetland. We know something, too, about the initiator of the enquiry, Thorvald Thoresson, Duke Håkon Magnusson's governor in Shetland, who probably lived in Papa Stour. Thorvald was a formidable man. His exploits were still remembered in the island half a millennium later.[33]

At Easter in 1299 a woman called Ragnhild Simunsdatter slandered Thorvald in Papa Stour, or so he reckoned. At the head court, probably a few months later, he called witnesses to report what she had said. The officials took the matter seriously: almost certainly Thorvald was hovering in the background. They even cut up one of his old letters to make their seal-tags; so there can be little doubt that Thorvald was in charge. Then they sent the letter to Duke Håkon.

The 1299 letter has potential to throw a flood of light on Shetland society at the end of the high middle ages. But it isn't easy to understand. It enters into exquisite detail about Ragnhild's alleged slanders, and even reports them, and Thorvald's retorts, in the protagonists' own words. But it's hard to understand their repartee, because we don't know who Ragnhild was, or what her interest was in the debate, and because all the parties used a difficult and specialised vocabulary.

---

32. For the text see Appendix, pp.81-2, *infra*.
33. George Low, *A Tour through the Islands of Orkney and Schetland* [1774], Kirkwall 1879, p.123: 'On a small level green, near the middle of the cultivated part [of Papa Stour], observed the marks of a circular enclosure, in which tradition says a Lord Terwil fought a duel with another gentleman, on some dispute or other, and afterwards accompanied by his eleven sons, went down on purpose to rob his neighbours, but together with his whole family perished on a rock, since called Terwil's Ba' or rock'.

'You shan't be my Judas'

Ragnhild and Thorvald locked horns in the living room of the duke's house in Papa Stour on the Monday of Passion Week, with a few Shetlanders looking on.

Figure 2 Bragister, Papa Stour: the bone of contention between Ragnhild Simunsdatter and Thorvald Thoresson in 1299. *Copyright Robert Crawford*

Ragnhild complained that Bragister, a small marginal farm on the south-east corner of the island (see Figure 2) was not, as she said, 'rented out as part of the "scat land" of the house'. 'The duke', she insisted, 'should take full rent even though Bragister were not included'. So their dispute was about *landskyld*, land-rent.[34]

Thorvald replied sharply. 'So many good men have dealt with this,' he said, 'such as Thorkell in Nes, Sir Eirik, Archdeacon Sigurd, Sir Eindrid, and many other able men who had full authority from my lord the duke concerning the sort of rent they took for him in Papa formerly'. But Ragnhild wasn't having any of it. Addressing the whole company she said: 'I gave no heed to the mad Eindrid, who ran away from Norway here and never knew a day's happiness; but all of you who knew have deceived the duke!'

The argument resumed on Tuesday. Ragnhild met Thorvald in the field outside the duke's house, and this time she didn't mince her words. To the astonishment of a priest and a Shetlander who were gawping she said to Thorvald: 'You shan't be my Judas, though you be Judas to the duke!'

Later in the year Thorvald brought up the matter at Shetland's lawthing, the head court of the islands. After sifting the evidence the officials made their adjudication on the question between Ragnhild and Thorvald. This is what they said: 'There has never been greater payment from the whole of Papa than that which has been

---

34. These events happened on 13-14 April 1299. Ingvild Øye pointed out at the Papa Stour conference in July 1999 that mid-April was the beginning of the northern summer: the term when land-rent was due. Cf. Magnus Lagabøter's Landlaw VII.1: 'skal landskylld uera firir sumarmal': 'land-rent shall be (paid) before summer': R. Keyser and P.A. Munch, *Norges Gamle Love indtil 1387*, ii, Christiania 1848, p.105.

common from of old: there is a mark of burnt gold for every cultivated "pennyland", and in rent 1½ "mælar" from every mark burnt: and there are then two "sáld" on every "pennyland".'

So the dispute was, as I said, about land-rent, levied on land-units called pennylands and marks of land – units unknown in Norway – and paid using standard Norwegian weights and measures called 'mælar' and 'sáld'. There is also talk of a parallel valuation of land in marks of burnt or pure gold and silver. These are deep waters!

But despite the problems I think we can work out what was going on in Papa Stour that Easter. We can do so by looking closely at Shetland's fiscal arrangements at the turn of the seventeenth and eighteenth centuries, and by contrasting and comparing them with those that feature in the 1299 letter. And we also have to consider Norway's equivalent institutions of 1299, which were different from Shetland's, but resembled them as well.

I argue that our document captures for us, in a vivid but cryptic way, how Shetland society was changing sharply on the eve of the late middle ages.

'The forsaid island being divided in four parts'

In November 1709 Patrick Mouat, the proprietor of Papa Stour, gave some land in the island to his sons. The way he described that land is vital for our purpose: 18 marks of land 'belonging to the roum of Gaurdie ... the forsaid island being divided in four parts, quhairof three lasts of land pertaining to Gaurdie forsaid'.[35]

From this document, and from other Mouat papers about the island,[36] we learn that the arable land of Papa Stour was divided into quarters; that each of the quarters was divided into three blocks called 'lasts of land', making 12 lasts of land in all; and that every last of land comprised 18 'marks of land'. Each mark of land was about an acre of arable land in extent.

Three of the quarters comprised the oldest arable land in the island, and were called Uphoose, Northoose and Sudderhoose. The fourth, incorporating half a dozen satellite or marginal farms (including Bragister, which Ragnhild had argued about with Thorvald in 1299) had the artificial name 'Gardie'.

This division of arable land into blocks called 'lasts of land', or occasionally 'half-lasts', was standard in every part of Shetland, provided that the host township was big enough to incorporate it. The block often took its name from a house in the township – Sudderhoose, Northoose, Uphoose – and seems to have been devised to prevent excessive fragmentation of the land tilled. Like communities everywhere in northern Europe Shetlanders divided their arable land into strips; but the Shetlanders tried to keep the inevitable fragmentation at bay by dividing their large townships into two or more fields. (For much more about this subject see Chapter 2, *infra*.) In other words, landlords and tenants held their shares in confined local spaces, to prevent the inevitable splitting from going too far. In the sixteenth and seventeenth centuries this or that holding in Shetland is thus often said to lie 'under the house of

---

35. National Archives of Scotland, RD.4/131, registered 10 January 1722: Disposition by Patrick Mowat of Hamnavoe to James Mowat and Robert Mowat, 9 November 1709.
36. See Note on sources and anomalies, pp.16-18, *infra*.

X' in township 'Y'. Papa Stour was so fertile that the last-blocks were especially big: they comprised three lasts of land each. Individual lasts in the three-last blocks of the island seem to have had names as well, also taken from a house: one of the three lasts of land of Uphoose, for instance, was called Uthascoll, from Old Norse *skáli*, a hall. [37]

The *purpose* of the Shetland last of land is clear: it was a tool for dividing land, and neatly accommodating the shares of tenants and landlords. I come now to its *origin*. We have seen that a last of land contained 18 or so marks of land: about 18 arable acres. But lasts of land in different places in Shetland diverged in the numbers of marks of land they contained. In Fair Isle we find eight 12-mark lasts;[38] in Bigton in Dunrossness four 16-mark lasts;[39] in Sandness and Papa Stour 18-mark lasts;[40] at Broo in Dunrossness six 24-mark lasts.[41] The difference between these lasts of land with variable marks of land was that each paid a different rate of rent per mark of land. Thus the 12-mark lasts paid 12 pennies, a shilling of rent, each; the 16-mark lasts ninepence per mark; the 18-mark lasts eightpence per mark; the 24-mark lasts sixpence per mark.[42] The significant point about these different lasts of land should be obvious: each of them, however many marks of land they comprised, paid 144 pennies or 12 shillings in rent. And in the old Orkney and Shetland system of weights and measures a last of goods was valued at 144 pennies. In other words, Shetland's lasts of land had their origin in, and acquired their strange name from a system of rent-assessment.

VARIOUS LASTS OF LAND IN SHETLAND

Fair Isle
8 lasts land of 12 marks land each,
each mark land paying rent at 12 pennies
= 144 pennies = 1 last of rent

Dale, Delting
2 lasts land of 18 marks land each,
each mark land paying rent at 8 pennies
= 144 pennies = 1 last of rent

Bigton, Dunrossness
4 lasts land of 16 marks land each,
each mark land paying rent at 9 pennies
= 144 pennies = 1 last of rent

Burrafirth, Unst
1 last land of 24 marks land each,
each mark land paying rent at 6 pennies
= 144 pennies = 1 last of rent

---

37. National Archives of Scotland, RS.45/6/2, folio 293: Instrument of sasine in favour of Patrick Mowat of Hamnavoe younger, 24 June 1702, following charter of 10 February 1699.
38. 'Fairisle 8 last land at 12 merk the last' (Gardie House, Bressay: Copy of rental of Yetland for Capt. Robert Wood, 1651).
39. 'my saxtein merk uthell land, nyn d. the merk, with the pertinentis in Scaitishous, comptit ane last of land' (Shetland Archives, GD.144/185/14: Disposition by James Sinclair of Goit to John Stewart, 9 November 1624).
40. 'ane last of udale land, extending to aughtene merk land, aught penneis the merk, in the toune of Melbie' (National Archives of Scotland, RS.43/2, folio 233: Instrument of sasine in favour of Patrick Cheine of Valey and Janet Gifhart his spouse, 28 March 1632).
41. 'last of land callit Vestagarth, extending to tuentie four merk land, lyand in the toune and landis of Brow' (National Archives of Scotland, RS.43/2, folio 255: Renunciation and discharge in favour of Andrew Bruce of Mowanes, etc., 13 June 1633).
42. The fact that lasts of land could contain variable numbers of marks of land was still understood by Thomas Edmondston in the mid-nineteenth century: *An Etymological Dictionary of the Shetland and Orkney Dialect*, Edinburgh 1866 ('last').

We must look closely at the pennies[43] and shillings of rent involved in these equations. They were a Shetland currency, payable not in coins but in goods,[44] paralleled in its details only by an identical system in Orkney. 12 Shetland pennies went to a Shetland shilling, and 12 Shetland shillings – 144 pennies – was a Shetland mark. The Shetland and Orkney mark was thus different from the sterling and Scots marks, which went for 13s.4d., and from any known Scandinavian mark. In Shetland at least it was long-lived: Shetlanders were still counting with their local 12-shilling mark as late as 1538.[45]

In other words, a last of land in Shetland paid in rent a last of goods; and a last of goods was worth 12 shillings or a Shetland mark.

Pennylands, marks of land

But what does all this have to do with our document of 1299, or Ragnhild's altercation with Thorvald Thoresson? At first sight the units and currency of the 1299 letter, especially its 'pennylands', look entirely different from those of our later systems. Shetland's pennylands have entirely disappeared by the seventeenth century; in fact they never appear in a Shetland document again after 1299.

This isn't surprising. Between 1299 and 1699 Shetland, like all the societies of northern Europe, had passed through the crucible of the Black Death and the late medieval depressions. In Norway valuation units of early modern times are different from their medieval predecessors, because of the unprecedented disruption after 1348.[46] In fact it's arguable that the Shetland units, despite their names, showed more stability than their Norwegian counterparts. Ragnhild and Thorvald wouldn't have had much difficulty in finding their way round Shetland's fiscal set-up in 1699.

So what is a pennyland? as F.W.L. Thomas famously enquired. We must now turn our attention to Orkney. In the nineteenth century Orcadians still divided up their arable land in pennylands, 18 of which made up an 'ounceland'. Many bold statements have been uttered about these Orkney units. Some historians[47] have argued, or rather stated, that they were Pictish in origin; others that they were designed to furnish conscripts for the navy; yet others that tax collectors created them to exact taxes for kings or popes. In fact they were primarily units for dividing up land, like Shetland's lasts and marks of land, and used – later – for myriad purposes (such as taxation).

18 pennylands in Orkney (and, I shall argue, in Shetland), made an ounceland. Why? In all the northern lands a mark was divided into eight ounces. As we've seen, the Shetland mark was valued at 144 pennies or 12 shillings. So an ounce – an eighth of it – contained 18 pennies. And therefore an ounceland contained 18 pennylands. We've already seen that Shetlanders still used a 12-shilling mark in the

---

43. In Orkney a last comprised 24 meils; a meil = six settings = six pennies: Hugh Marwick, *Orkney Farm-Names*, Kirkwall 1952, pp.195, 200. For Shetland see footnote 8, *infra*.
44. See 'Shetland's coinless currency, 1300-1700', p.xvi, *supra*. For a classic account of such currencies see Marc Bloch, 'Natural economy or money economy: a pseudo-dilemma', in *Land and Work in Medieval Europe*, London 1967, pp.230-43.
45. See 'Shetland's coinless currency, 1300-1700', p.xvi, *supra*.
46. Asgaut Steinnes, 'Mål, vekt og verderekning i Noreg i millomalderen og ei tid etter', in *Nordisk Kultur*, xxx, 1936, pp.142ff.
47. See Introduction, p.xi, *supra*.

sixteenth century; now we find that Orcadians had had a mark of the same value centuries previously.

> 1 Shetland/Orkney (and Cologne) mark = 144 pennies
> 1 mark everywhere = 8 ounces
> ∴ 1 Shetland/Orkney ounce = 144 ÷ 8 = 18 pennies
> ∴ 1 Shetland/Orkney ounceland = 18 pennylands

What was the origin of this unusual northern mark? The only possible model for it, as far as I can see, was the mark of Cologne, also worth 12 shillings or 144 pennies, which flourished in northern Europe in the eleventh and twelfth centuries.[48] That chronology fits beautifully with its presence in both Orkney and Shetland, whose institutions grew apart after Shetland was removed from the earldom of Orkney in 1195.

Peter Spufford gives a lucid account of European marks and their pennies:[49]

> [T]he mark became a unit of account at a time when the deniers [pennies] of Europe were marked by extreme diversity. The mark as a unit of account therefore came to mean different things in different places. In England and Scotland the mark or merk came to mean 13s.4d. (160 pence), in Cologne it came to mean 12s. (144 pfennigs), and by extension it was used to mean 144 pfennigs in neighbouring cities such as Aachen or Duisburg. In Lübeck, and thence in many other Hanseatic cities, it came to mean 16s. (192 pfennigs). However in Bremen it meant 32s. (384 pfennigs). In Denmark, Norway, Sweden and Gotland the mark was divided into 8 øre and 24 ørtug, but the number of pence to the ørtug varied. In Denmark and Norway there were 10, but in Sweden 8 and in Gotland 12. In Prussia the mark was divided into 24 skot, each of 30 pfennigs, making 720 pfennigs in all. Each of these meanings for the mark as a unit of account derived from a period when this many actual pence or pfennigs had been struck from a mark weight of silver. Such a period had to be long enough for the relationship to become customary. It was then fossilised for accounting purposes long after the real number of pence or pfennigs to the mark weight had eventually changed.

But why did the Orkney and Shetland mark have to have a model? Might it not have been local and unique? Spufford:[50]

---

48. The classic account is Walter Hävernick, *Der Kölner Pfennig im 12. und 13. Jahrhundert*, Stuttgart 1930, pp.43-9; cf. Pamela Nightingale, 'The evolution of weight standards and the creation of new monetary and commercial links in Northern Europe from the tenth century to the twelfth century', *Economic History Review*, xxxviii, 1985, p.200, and Harald Witthöft, 'Die Kölner Mark zur Hansezeit', in Michael North ed., *Geldumlauf, Währungssysteme und Zahlungsverkehr in Nordwesteuropa 1300-1800*, Köln 1989, pp.59ff. I am grateful to Pamela Nightingale and Harald Witthöft for advice concerning these matters.
49. Peter Spufford, *Money and its Use in Medieval Europe*, Cambridge 1998, p.223.
50. *Money and its Use*, pp.413-14. It is pretty futile to ask exactly when and why Shetlanders and Orcadians adopted the Cologne mark and its subdivisions for their currency, if that is what they did. There is, indeed, one vestige of a relationship between the islands and Germany in the eleventh century. According to Orkneyinga Saga, Earl Thorfinn Sigurdsson visited Emperor Henry III around 1048, en route to to Rome. Thorfinn 'then gave up warring-cruises, and turned his mind to the government of his land and people, and to the making of laws' (Alexander Burt Taylor ed., *The Orkneyinga Saga*, Edinburgh 1938, pp.188-9). Such a source is a slender basis for speculation about the metrological history of the islands. Nonetheless, an adoption of the Cologne mark in Orkney and Shetland in the later part of Thorfinn's reign might make good chronological sense. Gareth Williams has made the point that Thorfinn's known links with the archbishopric of Hamburg-Bremen would give him access to German's well-developed monetary economy (D.G.E. Williams, 'Land assessment and military organisation in the Norse settlements in Scotland, c.900-1266 AD', unpublished university of St Andrews Ph.D., 1996, p.132).

> The misnomer 'imaginary money' has often been applied to late-medieval money of account, perhaps because the real coin on which the money of account was resting was not always evident on first inspection. ... [I]t may be taken as axiomatic that on closer inspection an historical explanation may be found for the existence of each money of account, and that such an historical explanation will indicate to which real coin the system continued to be attached.

Shetland and Orkney had another land unit in common: the mark of land. We find this unit in the 1299 letter too,[51] and it can't be said to be obsolete in Shetland even today. The lawthingmen of Shetland said in 1299 that a cultivated pennyland was valued at a mark of burnt gold. A mark of burnt gold was the same as eight silver marks: in other words, each pennyland in the island had been revalued at some stage as eight marks of land. This is exactly how we find Orkney land described in rentals of the fifteenth and sixteenth centuries.[52] In other words, the revaluation of pennylands in both groups of islands as marks of land probably took place before 1195 as well. These marks of land were so-called because a mark was their purchase-price. Incredibly, Shetlanders were still buying and selling an average mark of land for a mark of goods as late as the 1620s.[53]

Let me sum up the story so far. In the seventeenth century Shetlanders divided their arable land into lasts of land and marks of land. In 1299 they divided the same land in pennylands and marks of land. Now I go on to ask: what is the link and the difference between the two?

'There has never been greater payment from the whole of Papa than that which has been common from of old'

At this point I wish to pay tribute to my long-suffering mathematics teacher and headmaster Bill Rhind, who I'm pleased to say is still with us, in his 93rd year. Bill often annotated my algebra notebook with the pithy statement: 'not a proper proof'. He did so because I habitually answered mathematical problems by thinking of the answer first: a bad habit, which I gather David Blunkett is still trying to extirpate. But I'm going to use that method again, to try to link the pennylands and marks of land of 1299 with the lasts of land of 1699.

The key sentence in the 1299 letter that enables us to do so, I propose, is the one with which the lawthingmen of Shetland concluded their public letter:

> There has never been greater payment from the whole of Papa than that which has been common from of old: there is a mark of burnt gold for every cultivated pennyland, and in rent 1½ mælar from every mark burnt: and there are then two sáld on every pennyland.

---

51. Strictly speaking there is no reference to a mark of land in the document. Instead we have a reference to a (re)valuation of the pennylands in marks of gold. But the mark of land, which features in Shetland documents from 1307 onwards (*Diplomatarium Norvegicum*, i, no. 109) - is *implicit* in the 1299 text, as we shall see.
52. In Henry Lord Sinclair's rental of Orkney of c.1500 there are a good many occasions when the number of marks in a pennyland is especially noted (Alexander Peterkin, *Rentals of the Ancient Earldom and Bishoprick of Orkney*, Edinburgh 1820, section 1, pp.10, 13, 16, 18, 26-9, 31, 35-6, 38-9, 44-5, 56-9, 61-3, 75, 77). At Ska in Deerness (p.10), and elsewhere, we find exactly the same mark-value for a pennyland that we found in Papa Stour in 1299: 'And to remember that ther is viij merk in ilk pennie terre of Ska supra'.
53. See 'Shetland's coinless currency, 1300-1700', p.xvii, *supra*, and Appendix, p.32, *infra*.

As we've seen, the lawthingmen were saying that each pennyland in Papa Stour was valued at eight marks of pure silver: eight marks of land. They also said that each mark of land paid 1½ mælar in rent, and that by definition each pennyland therefore paid two sáld, that is, eight times 1½ mælar, since six mælar went to a sáld.

These rent-payments of 1299 were made in corn, unlike Shetland's seventeenth century rents, which were paid in cloth ('wadmal') and butter. (This change is not surprising: Shetlanders can never have had much corn to spare, and the mode of payment was no doubt altered during the late medieval depressions.[54]) The corn-measurements of the 1299 letter, mælar and sáld, were absolutely standard Norwegian measurements of the time, and the relationship between them, six to one, was the rate set down by King Magnus Lagabøter in his great law-code of 1274.[55]

So each mark of land in Papa Stour in 1299 paid 1½ mælar of corn in rent. The word 'meil' was still in use in minor contexts in sixteenth and seventeenth century Shetland; but in Orkney, that fertile corn-growing country, it was still a basic corn-measurement as late as the nineteenth century. And the key point, for our purposes, is that in sixteenth century Orkney a meil of corn was worth six Orkney pennies (see footnote 43, *supra*). In Shetland too, in the seventeenth century, a meil of butter and oil, or rather an abstract combination of the two, were valued at six pennies.[56] In 1299 tenants of a mark of land in Papa Stour paid 1½ mælar of corn in rent; in the seventeenth century their descendants paid 10.6 ells (5.3 'pennies') of cloth and 10.6 marks (another kind of mark!) (2.6 'pennies') of butter. But each payment had much the same value – nine pennies or eight pennies respectively – in Shetland's old penny-currency.

I now take my leap into the dark. If I had been assessing the lands of Papa Stour in, say, the eleventh century, I would have assessed them as one ounceland: 18 pennylands. That isn't as wild as it seems. The ounceland was the basic building block of land assessment in medieval Orkney, and there is no reason to doubt that it was equally current in Shetland.[57] And there can be no debate about what land in Papa Stour would have been the original assessed land: the ancient arable land at Da Biggins. This is what Ragnhild called 'the scat land of the house' in 1299: probably there was an old original house there (which gave its name to Hoosa Voe). There were no doubt peripheral farms in the island: Bragister, Olligert, Evrigert, and so on, with their typical marginal place-name elements '-setter' and '-gert'. But these

---

54. There is no reference to a sáld of corn in any Shetland document after 1299. There are, however, place-names where the word is preserved: fields throughout Shetland are called Da Soldian or Soldians – including the obsolete 'Soldan last' in the now-deserted township of Gert in Dunrossness (Shetland Archives, D.8/32/10: Scroll sasine in favour of John Bruce of Sumburgh, December 1769). There is even a sunken rock in the sea north of the island of Bressay called Da Soldian: presumably because its extremely steep sides resemble those of a corn barrel.
55. Magnus Lagabøter's Landlaw VIII.29, in R. Keyser and P.A. Munch, *Norges Gamle Love indtil 1387*, ii, Christiania 1848, p.166.
56. Thus in c.1628 we find the following statements: (a) '6 meillis, viz. 3 leispund butter, 3 bullis oyllie'; (b) 'Ilk meill of scat is j leispund butter or j bull oyllie'; and (c) 'sex pennyis butter makis ane leispund' (Appendix, p.83, *infra*). It seems that a meil of corn has been 'translated' into a lispund of butter, with regard to their Shetland penny-value: solely, it seems, for purposes of rent- and scat-payment. This is an extremely curious translation, since in Orkney six lispunds of butter = one meil, not six meils (Hugh Marwick, *Orkney Farm-Names*, Kirkwall 1952, p.195). It does, however, prove that there was a connexion – albeit a bizarre one – between Shetland rent-payment in corn and (later) butter.
57. Willie Thomson has reassured me (personal communication, 17 August 1999): 'I think that you do better than just "guess" that Papa Stour was 18 pennylands. ... [T]his was the normal assessment of similar bordland "bus" in Orkney; since the assessment was presumably made on behalf of the Orkney earls, it is reasonable to assume that it would be done in the same way.'

places wouldn't have been assessed. They would have been mere satellites of 'the house'. We don't know who established that house: perhaps it was one of the earls of Orkney. It may well have been an establishment like the Orkney 'bus' of the high middle ages, where aristocrats and their bailiffs commandeered labour from peripheral farms.[58]

We may be able to catch a glimpse now of what Ragnhild was so angry about. During the old regime in the island the ancient arable land alone had been assessed. And now, perhaps, there was a new arrangement, with a new allocation of rent that suddenly affected Bragister.

'Many good men have dealt with this'

I return now to the Shetland last of land, which, as I said, paid a mark of goods in rent. There is a splendid parallel to this unit in Norway: the markebol, 'a land-unit which in land-rent gave a mark, or goods to the value of a mark'.[59] The Norwegian markebol didn't comprise marks of land, and it was smaller than the Shetland last of land; but the idea behind both seems to have been identical.

My contention is that a new system of land assessment, replacing the pennyland, but incorporating the marks of land, was introduced to Shetland at the end of the thirteenth century. Under the new arrangement a collection of marks of land was gathered together to form a block of land which paid a last, sometimes half a last, of rent. There is nothing improbable about such an innovation. Under Magnus Lagabøter the renting of land, and notions of tenancy, became central in the Norwegian polity.[60] When Magnus's son Håkon became duke of Norway in 1273 he acquired Shetland as part of his appanage.[61] Håkon was no doubt anxious to introduce modern Norwegian ideas in this backward part of the dukedom.[62]

How did he do so? I suggest that he appointed a commission to devise an appropriate system of land assessment for Shetland: a system based on land-rent, using local land-units and terminology, but with the Norse markebol as a model. Remember what Thorvald said to Ragnhild in 1299: 'So many good men have dealt with this, such as Thorkell in Nes, Sir Eirikr, Archdeacon Sigurd, Sir Eindrid, and many other able men who had full authority from my lord the duke concerning the sort of rent they took for him in Papa formerly.' This sounds to me like a group of commissioners, very important people. No doubt they were unpopular or caused bafflement in Shetland, because of their task: 'I gave no heed to the mad Eindrid,' said Ragnhild scornfully, 'who ran away from Norway here and never knew a day's happiness ...'

---

58. J. Storer Clouston, 'The Orkney "bus"', *Proceedings of the Orkney Antiquarian Society*, v, 1926-7, pp.41-9.
59. Halvard Bjørkvik, 'Markebol', in *Kulturhistorisk Leksikon for Nordisk Middelalder*, xi, Copenhagen 1981, col. 441. A Norwegian markebol paid a 'forngild' mark in rent, which was one third of the value of a burnt mark. In other words, a last of land in Shetland paid three times as much (in goods) as a markebol in Norway. But Sigvald Hasund has pointed out (*Or Noregs Bondesoge: glytt og granskingar*, ii, Oslo 1944, p.125, and cf. pp.120-3) that in the Opplands, the inland districts of Norway north of Oslo, also under Håkon Magnusson's control, 'the rent-mark was three times as large' as the rent-mark in Telemark. I am grateful to Lars Ivar Hansen and Jørn Sandnes for guidance about this question. I have a strong impression that the burnt mark was even more entrenched in Shetland's institutions than in those of the mother country.
60. For a clear account see Knut Helle, 'Down to 1536', in Rolf Danielsen et al. eds., *Norway: a history from the Vikings to our own times*, Oslo 1995, pp.51ff.
61. Grethe Authén Blom, *Samkongedømme-Enekongedømme – Håkon Magnussons Hertugdømme*, Oslo 1972, p.40.
62. For speculation about Håkon's imposition of tax in Shetland see Chapter 3, p.39, *infra*.

Knut Helle has argued forcefully[63] that the men listed by Thorvald weren't commissioners at all, but rent-collectors, perhaps Shetlanders who separately visited Papa Stour on the duke's behalf over a series of years. It is true that there can be no certainty about this question. We should keep in mind, however, that Sir Eirik was probably the well-known abbot of Munkeliv monastery, and Archdeacon Sigurd almost certainly Eirik's contemporary the archdeacon of Shetland. I find it difficult to believe that these two important ecclesiastics, one based in Bergen and the other (presumably) in Orkney, had taken time out to collect Duke Håkon's rent in Shetland. Four very important people, plus 'many other able men', armed with 'full authority from my lord the duke concerning what sort of rent they took for him in Papa formerly', sounds to me more like a commission than a succession of individuals. It is noteworthy that Thorkell & Co. had authority 'concerning *what sort of rent* they took for [the duke] in Papa': '*huilika landskylld* þeir toko honom til handa i Papey' (my italics). This is different from saying simply that they *took* rent.[64]

Helle has himself stressed[65] that fixing 'the *leidang* tax ... according to the size of the *landskyld* involved valuing all the land in the country. ... In this way each holding got a fixed landskyld assessment.' Andreas Holmsen says[66] that 'there was an official estimate (the *boltal*), which was based on a survey of the property, for the benefit of both parties. This estimate was made for the precise purpose of fixing a normal *landskyld*.' I suggest that making such an estimate is precisely what Thorkell & Co. had been doing. There must have been commissions at work everywhere in Norway, to effect such valuations.

So what did the commissioners do (if they were commissioners)? I propose that they devised an assessment of Shetland's arable land according to the rent it paid. This need not have involved an *increase* in rent; in fact the lawthingmen of Shetland were adamant in 1299 that there had 'never been greater payment from the whole of Papa than that which has been common from of old'. But what it would have involved was the bringing of peripheral farms, hitherto unassessed, into the new system. That was the final straw for Ragnhild. Remember what she bawled: 'Bragister was not rented out as part of the "scat land" of the house, and the duke should take full rent even though Bragister were not included'. If I am right, Bragister was now paying two sáld of corn, about six bags of the stuff: something, the present occupant of Bragister tells me that it is perfectly capable of doing. (In fact, George Peterson tells me that Bragister could comfortably have produced about forty bags of corn – without knowing that in medieval Norway the rent usually formed about one-sixth of the gross output of a holding.[67]) But I don't suppose that any of these statistics would have mollified Ragnhild.

Perhaps the new regime in Papa Stour looked something like the regime in Figure 4.

---

63. At the Papa Stour conference in Lerwick in July 1999. Despite the fact that we disagree I have greatly profited from discussing this matter with Knut Helle.
64. I am grateful to Paul Bibire for discussion of this point.
65. Knut Helle, 'Down to 1536', in Rolf Danielsen et al. eds., *Norway: a history from the Vikings to our own times*, Oslo 1995, p.51. For the relationship between *leidang* and *landskyld* in Norway see footnote 156, *infra*.
66. Andreas Holmsen, 'Desertion of farms around Oslo in the late middle ages', *Scandinavian Economic History Review*, x, 1962, p.171.
67. Knut Helle, 'Down to 1536', in Rolf Danielsen et al. eds., *Norway: a history from the Vikings to our own times*, Oslo 1995, p.27.

Almost seamlessly the Papa of 1299 becomes the Papa of c.1650. The old 'scat land of the house', previously an ounceland, becomes nine lasts of land, divided into three 'houses' of three lasts of land each.[68] This is the area now called 'Da Biggins'. The satellite farms are made to form another six pennylands, or three lasts of land. I concede, as I said before, that my starting-point, an old assessment of Papa Stour at one ounceland, is a leap into the dark. But consider that the *strict arithmetic* of my procedure results in an assessment of most of the peripheral farms at exactly one pennyland, or one half-last of land, each.[69] I believe that that result adds credibility to my reconstruction.

In fact, it would be consistent with the lawthingmen's statements (1) that there was 'a mark of burnt gold for every cultivated pennyland' in Papa Stour, and (2) that there were 'two sáld on every pennyland' there, *that they were speaking about Bragister itself* – as would have been logical, since Ragnhild's complaint was about Bragister! In my reconstruction Bragister (1) comprises one pennyland or eight marks of land (= eight marks of burnt silver = one mark of burnt gold), and (2) pays two sáld of corn in rent.

WHAT THE LAWTHINGMEN SAID

[with my comments in square brackets]

1 pennyland in Papa Stour is valued at 1 gold mark

[1 gold mark comprises 8 silver marks]

each of the 8 marks of land in Papa Stour pays 1½ mælar of corn in rent

[∴ 8 marks of land pay 12 mælar of corn in rent]

[6 mælar = 1 sáld]

∴ 1 pennyland (= 8 marks of land) pays 12 mælar = 2 sáld of corn

[i.e. Bragister (= 8 marks of land) pays 2 sáld of corn]

---

68. Keep in mind that these land units closely resembled each other: 18 pennylands = an ounceland, 18 or so marks of land = a last of land. Switching from one set to the other would not have posed major difficulties.
69. In a document of 1661 Bragister and Setter in Papa Stour are explicitly said to be half-lasts of land (Instrument of sasine in favour of Margaret Sinclair, 12-13 and 4 March 1661, following charter of 23 January 1661: National Archives of Scotland, RS.3/1, folio 19).

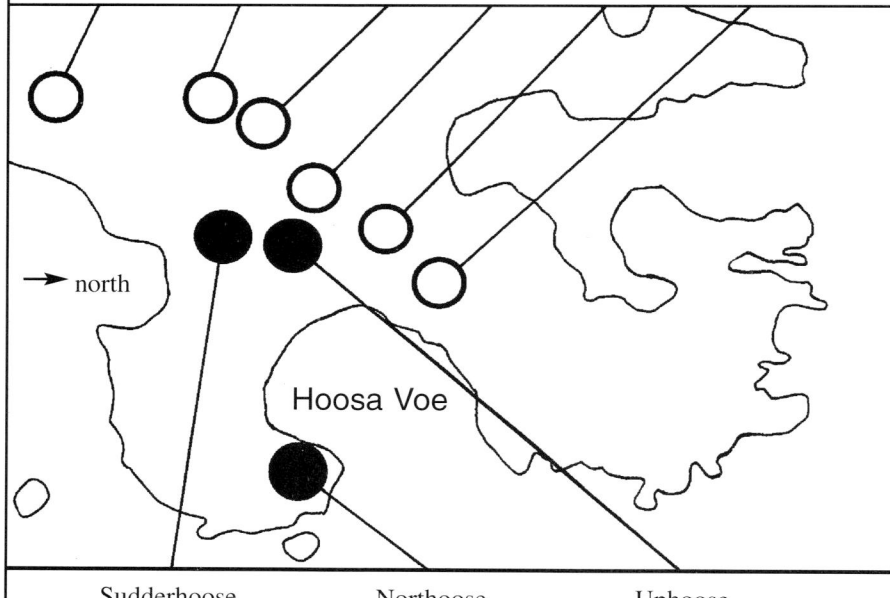

Figure 3 Papa Stour in c.1650. The sources for the information on this map are in the Note on sources and anomalies, *infra*, pp.16-18.

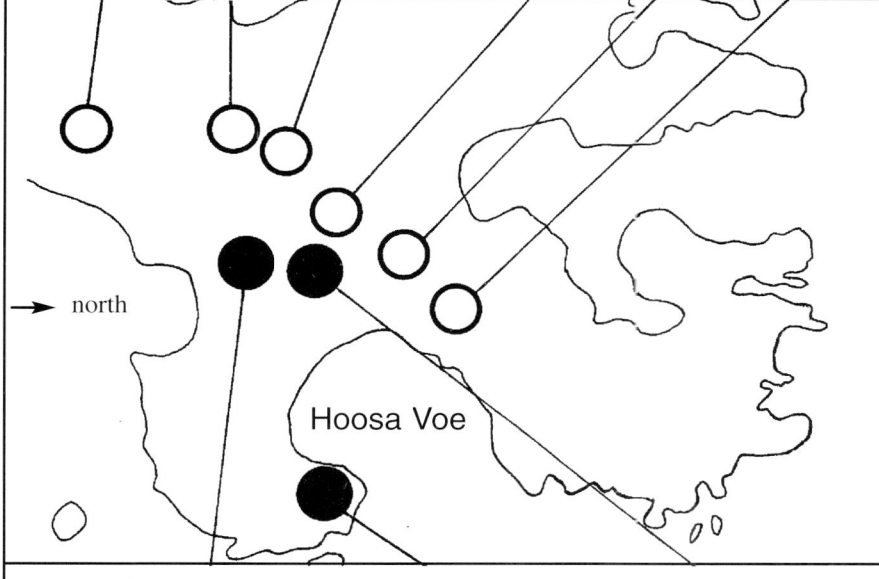

the satellite farms
6 pennylands, 48 marks of land, 3 lasts of land, paying 72 mælar corn in rent

Bragister	Mid Setter	Setter	Olligert	Hurdiback	Evrigert
1 pennyland	1 pennyland	1 pennyland	2 pennylands		1 pennyland
8 marks land	8 marks land	8 marks land	4 marks land	12 marks land	8 marks land
½ last land	½ last land	½ last land	1 last land		½ last land
12 mælar rent	12 mælar rent	12 mælar rent	6 mælar rent	18 mælar rent	12 mælar rent

Hoosa Voe

Sudderhoose	Northoose	Uphoose
6 pennylands	6 pennylands	6 pennylands
48 marks of land	48 marks of land	48 marks of land
3 lasts of land	3 lasts of land	3 lasts of land
72 mælar rent	72 mælar rent	72 mælar rent

the 'scat land of the house'
18 pennylands [= 1 ounceland], 144 marks of land, 9 lasts of land, paying 216 mælar corn in rent

PAPA STOUR in 1299?
24 pennylands, 192 marks of land, 12 lasts of land, paying 288 mælar corn in rent

Figure 4 Papa Stour in c.1299: a reconstruction

Propositions

I shall now summarise what I believe the 1299 letter about Papa Stour means, in five brief propositions.

1. Originally (I propose), the old arable land of Papa Stour was valued as an ounceland, whose 18 pennylands (valued at eight marks of land) eventually paid 12 mælar of rent each. Bragister and the other marginal farms of the island didn't pay a separate rent: they may have provided labour for the Papa manor.

2. At the very end of the thirteenth century a revaluation of Papa took place, under the auspices of Duke Håkon Magnusson, who sent a commission of 'good men' to Shetland to effect it.

3. As a result, all the arable land of Papa was revalued according to the amount of rent the island was deemed to be able to pay. The satellite farms now paid a separate rent. Under this revaluation the pennylands were increased in number from 18 to 24. A new series of units eventually called 'lasts of land' came into existence, rather like the pennylands, but named after the amount of rent they paid. These units were modelled on the markebol of Eastern Norway.

4. Ragnhild Simunsdatter, whoever she was, had fixed views about the new arrangement. During altercations with Thorvald Thoresson, the duke's agent in the islands, she contended:

(a) that Bragister shouldn't pay a rent separate from the rent of the main house (or Uphoose), because it hadn't in the past; and

(b) that Thorvald was cheating the duke by collecting more rent from Papa than hitherto – and, presumably, putting the surplus in his pocket. Hence Ragnhild's use of the word 'Judas'.[70]

5. But Thorvald's contention, made in reply to Ragnhild, and subsequently sent to Norway for the duke's benefit, was that the revaluation hadn't resulted in higher *rates* of rent in Papa. He argued that Bragister now paid a separate rent of 2 sáld of corn, *albeit at the old rate*, following the revaluation.

Is it as simple, and as complicated, as that?

*

'The retrospective method is always dangerous'.[71] It can certainly lead to wishful thinking and error. There is peril in assuming that institutions of 1299 and 1699 were the same, or much the same. But my assumption isn't that there was stasis in Shetland during those four centuries. I contend that by reconstructing the rural landscape of the islands in the thirteenth century we can better understand how Shetland society changed later.

By looking at the fiscal material from Papa Stour, and comparing it with, say, Clouston's and Thomson's work on medieval landscapes in Orkney,[72] we can

---

70. Ragnhild's likening of Thorvald to Judas was perhaps a little strong. Ananias (Acts 5) might have been more apposite! Note, however, that in 1395 Bishop Eystein of Oslo called the people of Telemark Judases for betraying the then king (*Diplomatarium Norvegicum*, ix, no. 186). Willie Thomson has suggested to me that Ragnhild may have had Judas in mind because it was Easter.
71. Léopold Genicot, *Rural Communities in the Medieval West*, Baltimore 1990, p.16.
72. J. Storer Clouston, 'The Orkney "bus"', *Proceedings of the Orkney Antiquarian Society*, v, 1926-7, pp.41-9; William P.L. Thomson, 'Settlement patterns at Tuquoy, Westray, Orkney', in *Northern Studies*, xxvii, 1990, pp.35-49; William P.L. Thomson, 'Some settlement patterns in medieval Orkney', in Colleen Batey et al. eds., *The Viking Age in Caithness, Orkney and the North Atlantic*, Edinburgh 1993, pp.340-8.

pinpoint the moment when change happened. The manors of aristocrats (not very numerous in Shetland, I grant you) were dissolving and splitting up into individual farms, separately assessed and tenanted by free men and women. These are the farms we find in documents of the seventeenth century, assessed in ways which must have been devised in the middle ages.

There is value, too, in comparing and contrasting our rent systems and methods of land division of the thirteenth and seventeenth centuries. Not because it is exciting to see continuities – that really is the cheapest kind of antiquarian thrill – but because of the striking and subtle *mutations* that the comparison reveals. Shetlanders were still dividing and redividing their arable land as lasts and half-lasts of land in the late eighteenth century, as we shall see in Chapter 2. But their attempts to impose a rational structure on the landscape were by then flagging. As the population of the islands exploded, and the islands' fisheries became more complex and specialised, fragmentation of property became unstoppable. Shetland's old fixed rents, current for half a millennium, quickly ceased to exist.

These institutions and relationships, their waxing and waning, were at the very heart of social life in Shetland. They enshrined the way that men and women thought about their homes and settlements: how they valued them, measured them, divided them, leased them, sold them and levied tax on them. 'Contemptible details these, to make part of a history, yet the turn of most lives is hardly to be accounted for without them.'[73]

---

73. George Eliot, *Daniel Deronda*, 1876, chapter 21.

A note on sources and anomalies

There is a great deal of documentary material extant about the division of Papa Stour into (1) quarters, (2) lasts of land and (3) marks of land, and about (4) the amount of rent paid by each of the marks of land in Shetland pennies. These documents almost all date from the period around 1700.

(1) *Quarters.* In 1709 Patrick Mowat stated that Papa was 'divided in four parts'.[74]

(2) *Lasts of land.* Each of the quarters comprised three lasts of land: (a) 'thrie lasts of land in Northous, thrie lasts of land in Sutherhous, thrie lasts of land in Uphous';[75] and (b) three lasts of land in 'Gairdie'.[76] As confirmation of this Papa is frequently stated to comprise 12 lasts of land.[77]

(3) *Marks of land.* In Thomas Gifford's rental of 1716 Papa is said to comprise 216 marks of land. This implies 12 lasts of 18 marks of land each.[78] As confirmation of this Patrick Mowat states in 1715 that his three lasts of land in Uphouse and three lasts of land in 'Garden' 'comprehend ... eighteen merk land to each last'.[79]

(4) *Pennies paid per mark of land in rent.* According to documents of 1697 and 1699 the three lasts of 'Gardie', 1½ lasts of land in Sudderhoose and the last of land called Uthascoll in Uphoose, paid rent at eight pennies per mark of land.[80] This strongly suggests that in the seventeenth century all the lasts of Papa comprised 18 marks of land, paying rent of eight pennies per mark of land: 144 pennies or a last of goods in rent per last of land (the original rent paid by a last of land).

In two documents of 1698, however, we find information which does not at first sight conform with this neat picture:

(1) A disposition by Margaret Mowat to James Mowat her son, 31 March 1698, of 12 marks of land in Bragasiter, 12 marks of land in Midsetter and 12 marks of land in Seatter, all paying rent at eight pennies per mark of land;[81] and

(2) An instrument of sasine, 9 June 1698, in favour of Hector Mowat, following disposition by Margaret Mowat, 6 April 1698, of 18 marks of land in Hurdiback, 12 marks of land in Avragarth and six marks of land in 'normost house of Ollagarth', all paying rent at eight pennies per mark of land.[82]

The six places dealt with in these documents, comprising 72 marks of land,

---

74. National Archives of Scotland, RD.4/131, registered 10 January 1722: Disposition by Patrick Mowat of Hamnavoe to James Mowat and Robert Mowat, 9 November 1709.
75. Shetland Archives, D.24, bundle of Papa deeds: Instrument of sasine in favour of Patrick Mowat, 12 June 1711, following charter of 1 November 1710.
76. National Archives of Scotland, RS.45/6/2 fol. 397: Instrument of sasine in favour of Patrick Mowat of Ballwhally, 24 and 26 June 1702, following charter of 30 July 1697. 'Gardie' appears as 'Garden' on one occasion (Shetland Archives, D.24, bundle of Papa deeds: Wadset by Patrick Mowat of Balquhallie to Arthur Nicolson of Bulyeseter, 20 October 1711).
77. E.g. instrument of sasine in favour of Gilbert Mowat, 23-4 and 26-8 July 1624, following precept of chancery of 30 March 1624: A.W. and A. Johnston, *Orkney and Shetland Records,* ii, London 1907-42, p.44.
78. National Archives of Scotland, RH.9/15/176, p.51.
79. Shetland Archives, D.24, box 69, bundle 2: Wadset by Patrick Mowat of Balquhallie to Arthur Nicolson of Bulyeseter, 20 October 1711.
80. National Archives of Scotland, RS.45/6/2, folio 398: Instrument of sasine in favour of Patrick Mowat of Hamnavoe younger, 9 July 1702, following charter of 30 July 1697; and folio 293: Instrument of sasine in favour of Patrick Mowat of Hamnavoe younger, 24 June 1702, following charter of 10 February 1699.
81. Shetland Archives, GD.144/260/2.
82. Shetland Archives, GD.144/78/1.

paying rent at eight pennies per mark of land, make up the three lasts of land of 'Gardie'. But from the above information we would expect 54 marks of land (3x18), paying eight pennies per mark of rent, in 'Gardie', rather than 72.

It looks as if there have been four ways of describing the lasts of land of 'Gardie' over the centuries:

(1) In 1299 (see Figure 4) all the marks of land in Papa are said to pay 1.5 mælar corn in rent. 16 marks of land therefore pay 144 pennies = one last of rent. The three lasts of land of 'Gardie' therefore comprise 48 marks of land.

(2) By the mid-seventeenth century (see Figure 3) the three lasts of land of 'Gardie' pay rent at eight pennies the mark of land, as described in the charter of 30 July 1697 mentioned above. 18 marks of land therefore pay 144 pennies = one last of land. The three lasts of land of 'Gardie' therefore comprise 54 marks of land (as described above).

(3) During the seventeenth century these three lasts of land of 18 marks of land each, paying rent of eight pennies per mark of land, seem to have become three lasts of land of 24 marks of land, paying rent of six pennies per mark of land. This is a deduction: there is no documentary evidence for any payment of six pennies the mark of land in 'Gardie'. But such an apparently pointless change is well-documented elsewhere in Shetland. In the large islands of Unst and Fetlar, at an unknown date, *all* townships were reassessed as paying rent of six pennies per mark of land, with corresponding increases or reductions in the number of marks of land in them.[83]

Perhaps Shetland rents were reassessed in this way because six pennies = one meil.[84] Note that 'Gardie' paid 72 mælar of rent in corn (54 x 1.5 meils) in my reconstruction; hence, perhaps, a reassessment as 72 marks of land (x one meil).

The changes described in (1)-(3) above are tabulated below:

places	lasts of land	marks of land		
		9 pennies the mark	8 pennies the mark	6 pennies the mark
Bragister	½	8	9	12
Mid Setter	½	8	9	12
Setter	½	8	9	12
Olligert	¼	4	4.5	6
Hurdiback	¾	12	13.5	18
Evrigert	½	8	9	12
'Gardie'	3	48	54	72

Table 1 Rents of different rates per mark of land paid by places in 'Gardie'.

(4) The final change is the most radical: here the link between a last of land and a last of rent disappears. By 1698 the rent of the 72 marks of land in Gardie has been raised from six to eight pennies per mark of land. Instead of three lasts (432 pennies) 'Gardie' now pays four lasts of rent (576 pennies):

---

83. National Archives of Scotland, E.41/7, folios 10 and 12: Rental of Yetland of c.1628.
84. Lindsay Macgregor made this suggestion to me many years ago.

places	lasts of land	marks of land	rent at 6 pennies the mark	rent at 8 pennies the mark (1698)
Bragister	½	12	72p	96p
Mid Setter	½	12	72p	96p
Setter	½	12	72p	96p
Olligert	¼	6	36p	48p
Hurdiback	¾	18	108p	144p
Evrigert	½	12	72p	96p
'Gardie'	3	72	432p = 3 lasts	576p = 4 lasts

Table 2 Rents of six pennies and eight pennies per mark of land paid by places in 'Gardie'.

Increases or decreases in pennies of rent payable per mark of land are not unknown in Shetland in the seventeenth century.[85] In the case of 'Gardie' there was a good practical reason for an alteration upwards (from six to eight). By the nineteenth century Bragister and the other marginal farms in Papa, by then in the hands of the Gifford family, were regarded as relatively more valuable than the ancient arable land belonging to the Nicolson family at Da Biggins, presumably because runrig had not affected them so much.[86] In 1847, for instance, John Henry, a tenant in the island, told a court that 'Setter, Braggister, and Midsetter are the best towns in the island'. And William Henry, a native of Papa, said that 'the merks land of Papa were divided into 12 lasts of 18 merks each ... and that of the 12 lasts aforesaid *two-thirds* belong to Sir Arthur Nicolson, and the other *third* to Mr Gifford' (my italics). Strictly speaking Nicolson owned nine of the lasts of land (Da Biggins) and Gifford three ('Gardie'), but the higher rents at 'Gardie' made the latter look relatively large.[87]

---

85. E.g. 'Reirweik xj merk, xij d. the merk ... set be my lord [Earl Patrick Stewart] for ix d. merk' (National Archives of Scotland, E.41/7, folio 3: Rental of Yetland of c.1628).
86. Cf. what William Balfour wrote about the marginal farm of Littlaland in Fetlar in the 1770s: 'The arable, something above 11 acres, is of a very mean soil, and of 10 acres or more of pasture ground there is not much that is rich or good; yet it happens here, as almost every where in Shetland, that the sole tenant of the town, by superior industry, lives better and pays his rent more punctually than those that possess so much better land in the towns of Finzie, Strand and Aith, where many tenants are crowded together and labour run rigg. For it holds universally, the more extensive the town and the more farmers upon it, the poorer they are' (Shetland Archives, Hay & Co. Papers: Rental of Shetland c.1774).
87. Both quotations are from Appendix B in action of division of run-rig lands at instance of Sir Arthur Nicolson against Arthur Gifford of Busta and others, 13 July 1853, p.5: Shetland Archives, D.24, box 69, bundle of papers anent Papa division.

2
Lasts of land

A last was a measurement, usually of weight, sometimes of quantity. The quantities and weights were large, sometimes spectacularly so: 10,000 fish, for instance,[88] or several tons.[89] Lasts are obsolete now, but it isn't long since they were familiar throughout Northern Europe. They flourished from the high middle ages until relatively recent times, all over the place, from Frisia, their likely place of origin, to France.[90]

Goods weighed or counted in lasts were often contained in barrels, usually 12 of them at a time: butter and oil and similar 'fat goods' (as they were called in Shetland), corn, fish, beer, lime, iron.[91] Even empty barrels were counted in lasts. In 1639 some German merchants in Shetland paid three lasts of such barrels, in other words 36 of them, as part payment of their customs dues.[92] Everywhere we find a relationship between lasts and twelves: in the late sixteenth century Sir Jerom Horsey, recently returned from Russia, presented Queen Elizabeth with a last of hawks and a last of falcons, presumably a dozen each.[93]

Lasts were so big that they caught the public imagination. In Lang's fairy-tale 'Minnikin' there is a search for 'someone who could brew a hundred lasts of malt at one brewing, for there was to be a feast at the Troll's, at which less than that would not be drunk'.[94] There was a pub in Black Lion Street in Brighton originally known as the Last and Fishcart. 'Long time I've longed for good beer,' announced a sign outside, 'But at "The Last" I've found it here.'[95] Authors sometimes used the word figuratively to refer to huge amounts of this or that. During a delicious interlude between Chaucer's shipman's tale and the prologue of the prioress's tale the host suddenly announces: 'God yeve the monk a thousand last quade yeer!' (a thousand lasts of bad seasons).[96] And in 1581 Barnaby Rich, in his work *Farewell to Military Profession*, portrays a woman who welcomes her soldier husband home 'with a whole laste of kisses'.[97]

The lasts I write about here are less exciting than Rich's, but they are unique. Almost anything could be weighed or measured in lasts, from time to time; but

---

88. W.D. Parish, *A Dictionary of the Sussex Dialect and Collection of Provincialisms in use in the County of Sussex* [1875], Bexhill 1967, p.73.
89. *Parliamentary Papers* 1820, viii, report, p.21.
90. Elis Wadstein, 'Frisiska lånord', *Studier tillägnade Axel Kock*, Lund 1929, pp.406-7.
91. For a useful list of goods countable in lasts see Sam Owen Jansson, 'Om läst och lästetal', *Sjöhistorisk Årbok* (Stockholm), 1945-6, p.29.
92. National Archives of Scotland, GD.190/3/243/1, folio 3: 'Compt of ressait of the custumes toll and buleoun 1639'.
93. Edward A. Bond ed., *Russia at the Close of the Sixteenth Century*, London 1861, p.234.
94. Andrew Lang ed., *The Red Fairy Book*, London 1890, p.318.
95. *English Dialect Dictionary* ('Last').
96. Larry D. Henson ed., *The Riverside Chaucer*, Oxford 1988, p.208.
97. Thomas Mabry Cranfill ed., *Rich's Farewell to Military Profession 1581*, Austin, Texas 1959, p.145.

Shetlanders (I guarantee) were the only people anywhere in the world who had lasts of land.

'Acording to the number and quantitie of the lastis'
When we first meet lasts of land in Shetland documents, at the turn of the sixteenth century, it's clear that there were two species of them. For convenience I shall call them *arithmetical* and *practical* lasts of land. I deal with the arithmetical breed first.

Figure 5 Jeannie and Kirstie Blance rake soil over newly sown grain at Udhoose in Delting, in the 1930s (photograph by Robbie Williamson). *Copyright Shetland Museum.*

Every old township in Shetland was divided into marks of land (see Chapter 1, *supra*). The number of marks of land in a township remained fixed throughout the centuries, and the number of Shetland 'pennies' of rent that each paid remained stable and significant,[98] at least until about 1700. Throughout Shetland we find townships valued at 8, 9, 16, 18, 36, 54, 72 and as many as 144 marks of land, with many other variations. These are half-lasts, single lasts or multiple lasts of land, originally designed to furnish half-lasts (72 'pennies'), single lasts and multiple lasts of rent, and other duties for that matter,[99] to landlords and superiors.

---

98. For these 'pennies' see 'Shetland's coinless currency, 1300-1700', pp.xvi-xvii, *supra*. Early in the seventeenth century the number of pennies of rent paid by a mark of land could still be a vital matter. In the 1620s Ninian Neven of Windhouse forced Thomas Aiklay in Utrabister in Yell, 'ane pure simple feard man', to give him various lands: 'four merk land in Stiflour and ane half, sex pennyes the merk, and ane merk half merk land, ix d. the merk, in North Sandwik'. 'And in respect the half merk land wes nocht ix d. the merk,' complained Aiklay, '... he forst and compellit me to give him my best horse in recompence thairof' (*Register of the Privy Council of Scotland*, xiv, p.764).
99. Shetlanders of the sixteenth century paid entry-fines, and occasionally scat, according to the last of land. See John H. Ballantyne and Brian Smith eds., *Shetland Documents 1195-1579*, p.207: 'for ilk thre yeiris gerssowme of ane last of land thay war wont to pay fyve dolouris'. This agrees well with a statement of c.1550 that 'in Hieltland the tenant gives his landlord 6 "Hieltlenske" gylden every 3 years for every 18 marks of land, and that is called 'aasete köp"' (*Shetland Documents 1195-1579*, no. 91). In c.1510 'the southt last in Tresta' in Aithsting paid 14 'pennies' of cloth in scat, and 'the last in Schatsta' in Delting 19 ells of cloth-scat (*Shetland Documents 1195-1579*, pp.258, 260). Note that these scat-paying lasts were 'practical' rather than 'arithmetical'.

Lasts of land were extremely useful for facilitating various kinds of assessment in the islands. They were sometimes more serviceable for such purposes than the tiny marks of land. In July 1600, for instance, Earl Patrick Stewart's sheriff wrote to two officials in the island of Yell.[100] Patrick was hard up, as usual; he was trying to raise cash, probably for work on his new castle at Scalloway. 'Ye sall nocht faill', wrote Sheriff Dishington,

> to pas and collect the summe of [£5 6s.8d.] Scottis monie for ilk last of the haill landis within the yle of Yell ... acording to the number and quantitie of the lastis. And for tryell of the quantitie thairof ye sall tak advyse of Piter Nisbeit, Gilbert Nisbeit, Osie Scott, William Spens, James in Swaresetter, and John Nevebak; and in cais of ... thair absence ye sall try the quantitie of the lastis your selff ... with thame that ar present ...

In other words, the number of lasts of land in a given township were well-known in the parish, and well-remembered by local people.

Earl Patrick habitually used lasts of land to effect assessments and impose burdens. In July 1603 he decided that the people of Burra, an island near Scalloway, should provide a boat or boats in case he wanted goods moved or a handy ferry.[101] With customary generosity he gave them a choice. Either provide a rota of ferries, where 'ilk last land serve[s] alyk' – that is, where each last of land furnishes a boat whenever Patrick snaps his fingers – or provide a new boat, for Patrick's exclusive use. And then the following February, toasting in front of the fire at his palace of Birsay in Orkney, Patrick wrote a letter to his Shetland officials.[102] He instructed them to make arrangements for cutting peats for Scalloway Castle, presumably for use when Patrick came to Shetland in the summer, and to ensure that every three lasts of land in several given parishes cut and provide a fathom of peats. This doesn't seem very onerous until we discover that Earl Patrick's fathom was 20 feet high, 16 feet broad and 14 feet long.

Last-assessment persisted in Shetland after Patrick's regime faded away, and long afterwards. In 1612, for instance, Shetland's gentry clubbed together to provide a schoolmaster for their children. With a view to doing so they resolved to collect three shillings Scots from every last of land in the islands.[103] And in March 1650, when the Marquis of Montrose was landing in Orkney to spearhead his fateful campaign, the earl of Morton collected what he called a 'voluntarie subsederie' (or subsidy) of 12 shillings 'for ilke last of land' in Shetland, 'towardes', as he put it, 'the present expeditioune in hand'.[104] There was a Shetland law – one of the so-called 'Country Acts' – 'that none have more swine than four upon a last of land over winter, under the pain of 10 pounds.'[105] As late as the late eighteenth century an assessor in Sandwick, in the south mainland of Shetland, used the lasts of land in the

---

100. John H. Ballantyne and Brian Smith eds., *Shetland Documents 1580-1611*, Lerwick 1994, no. 300. Cf. also no. 353, where Patrick is said to have demanded an angel noble from each last of land in Shetland in 1599 and 1600.
101. Gordon Donaldson ed., *The Court Book of Shetland 1602-1604*, Edinburgh 1954, p.100.
102. John H. Ballantyne and Brian Smith eds., *Shetland Documents 1580-1611*, no. 378.
103. National Archives of Scotland, RD1/232, folio 256.
104. Shetland Archives, GD.144/114/19. A year later Captain Robert Wood collected duties throughout Shetland from the lasts of land: 'The soume of all the lasts of land given up to me be the severall baylies', he reported, 'exstends to the number of 596 lasts 6 merk' (Gardie House, Bressay: Copy of rental of Ye land for Capt. Robert Wood, 1651).
105. Thomas Gifford, *An Historical Description of the Zetland Islands* [1786], Sandwick 1976, p.84. For Shetland's Country Acts see pp.44 and 46, *infra*.

parish to organise work on the building of a new hill dyke. On that occasion the inhabitants of every last of land had to build 50 fathoms.[106]

These, then, are examples of the 'arithmetical' use of lasts of land in the islands. But there's no doubt at all that many lasts of land were visible and 'real' just as much as they were theoretical: they were large fields, probably of myriad shapes, within the confines of townships. They sometimes had names like the North or South Last,[107] the Great Last or the Small Last,[108] showing that they had a geographical reality. Often they took the name of a house in the township concerned. At Bigton in Dunrossness, for instance, there were four 16-mark lasts of land, called Breck, Scatshoose, Mews (the middle house) and Sinsthoose (the southmost house).[109] (We have already seen, in Chapter 1, that the lasts of Papa Stour were named in this way.) Another very good example is the arrangement in the smallish township of Culswick in the parish of Sandsting, valued at 36 marks of land (see Figure 6). In Culswick there was a North Last[110] and a South Last,[111] sometimes called the North and South Toons,[112] attached respectively to two houses called Northoose and Soothhoose.[113] Each of these Culswick lasts comprised 18 marks of land. On quite a few occasions, at Culswick and elsewhere, the arable land is said to lie 'under the house' of X in the township of Y, suggesting, once again, that a last of land was a field.

There are no lasts of land known by name or reputation in Shetland today. But we can, on a few occasions, spot where the boundaries of lasts must have been, from hints in documents or place-names. Culswick is a good example. It's not too long since the inhabitants of that little place were getting letters addressed either to North or South Culswick, sometimes to the mystification of younger members of the family. There is still a house there called Da Nort Toon by older people.[114] These clues enable us to spot the boundary between the erstwhile North and South Lasts: it was a straight line which neatly bisected the arable land of the place.

Similarly, at Brebister in the parish of Waas there were two lasts of land.[115] According to seventeenth century documents they lay 'benorth' and 'besouth' the

---

106. Shetland Archives, D.8/184.
107. E.g. the North Last of Setter in Waas (National Archives of Scotland, RS.44/2, folio 55: Instrument of sasine in favour of Harie Ollasoun of Seitter following disposition of 1 November 1624); and the South Last of Caldback in Delting (National Archives of Scotland, RS.44/2, folio 220: Instrument of sasine [16 February 1627] in favour of John Tullo in Cauldback).
108. E.g. the Great Last of Melby in Sandness (John H. Ballantyne and Brian Smith eds., *Shetland Documents 1580-1611*, Lerwick 1994, no. 274); and the Small Last in Exnaboe in Dunrossness (National Archives of Scotland, RS.44/2, folio 228: Instrument of sasine [16 January 1632] in favour of James Sinclair of Quendell).
109. Shetland Archives, GD.144/267/14: Disposition by Margaret Leask, relict of Laurence Sinclair of Goit, to John Stewart, 18 November 1626, of her liferent title and possession of 'ane last of land in Sinshous, all and haill ane last of land in Mewhous, all and haill ane last of land in Scatishous, comptand sextein merk land to ilk last', with 12 merks land 'in the town and lands of Breck'.
110. John H. Ballantyne and Brian Smith eds., *Shetland Documents 1580-1611*, Lerwick 1994, no. 423.
111. National Archives of Scotland, RS.44/3, folio 234: Instrument of sasine (3 December 1641) in favour of Patrik Umphray of Sand, following disposition of land 'in the rowme and lands of Cultiswick, in the south last thairof'.
112. National Archives of Scotland, RS.44/3, folio 198: Instrument of sasine (23 June 1640) in favour of John Mansone in Cultiswick, following disposition of 'all and haill his thrie merk land in the said south toun of Coultiswick'.
113. *Shetland Documents 1195-1579*, p.264: 'Item, the northt hous in Cullisuek, ... Item, the southt hous in Cullisuek ...' (c.1507x1513). As late as 1850 and 1853 respectively the land surveyor Thomas Irvine divided 'the North Town' and 'the South Town' of Culswick into six farms each: Shetland Archives, D.16/394/2, p.113.
114. I am grateful to Wilma Cluness and Mary Fraser for help about these matters.
115. 'The sutht last of Brabuster' and 'the north last of the samin' in a document of 1549: *Shetland Documents 1195-1579*, no. 88.

Figure 6 Culswick, Sandsting, photographed by Jack Rattar in the 1930s. This township comprised 36 marks of land. The 'South Last' is nearest the camera. *Copyright Shetland Museum.*

gait' or road.[116] At first sight there is no sign of a road there today, but older people can point out an ancient path which ran from Vesquoy in mid Waas for four miles or so as far as Doonawaas, the main settlement of the parish.[117] That path ran through the arable land of Brebister. No-one has heard of the north and south lasts of Brebister today, but thanks to the documents they can still be discerned in the landscape.

My final example is relatively intact even today. As I have said, the southmost last of Bigton in Dunrossness was called Sinsthoose, a name which survives only in a few seventeenth century documents. Sinsthoose is now simply called the Bigton Farm; but in the mid-eighteenth century it was called the Hall Last, after the manor house that the Bruce family had built there. In 1775 John Bruce Stewart of Symbister entered into a contract with his brother that [118]

> the farm called the Hall-last of Bigtoun, consisting of sixteen merk land, with the island of St Ninians, shall be kept and reserved to the parties themselves, and be managed by the said William Bruce, the said island to be used for grasing of slaughter cattle, milk cows and sheep, ... and the said sixteen merk land to be kept and used as a farm.

---

116. E.g. National Archives of Scotland, RS.44/2, folio 207: Instrument of sasine in favour of Robert Colt, following disposition by Sara Wischard of 8 February 1631, of 'all and haill that hir four merk udalland, aught pennies the merk, in Brabister besouth the gait'.
117. I am grateful to Christie Fraser for this information.
118. Shetland Archives, GD.144/118/16.

'You will have to make a very complicated reckoning'

We now have to ask: why did Shetlanders divide their townships into these blocks of arable land? The answer seems to have to do with the tendency of plots of arable land in this kind of society to split into innumerable small fields, and the way that Shetlanders tried to keep that tendency at bay. Here I want to quote a sparkling passage from the Russian medievalist Paul Vinogradoff, which sums up the problems and dilemmas which Shetlanders and others faced when they organised their land.

'The territory of the township', says Vinogradoff,[119]

> is not like a homogeneous sheet of paper out of which you may cut lots of every desirable shape and size: the tilth will present all kinds of accidental features, according to the elevation of the ground, the direction of the watercourses and ways, the quality of the soil, the situation of dwellings, the disposition of wood and pasture-ground, etc. The whole must needs be dismembered into component parts, into smaller areas or furlongs, each stretching over land of one and the same condition, and separated from land of different quality and situation. Over the irregular squares of this rough chess-board a more or less entangled network of rights and interests must be extended.

What Vinogradoff is describing here is the practice of subdividing settlements into small strips, absolutely standard in medieval and sometimes post-medieval rural communities, from the far west to the far east. In Scotland we call it runrig; in Shetland rigga-rendal or rig aboot.

'There seem to be only two ways of doing it', continues Vinogradoff.

> You may simply give every householder a share in every one of the component areas, and subject him in this way to all the advantages and drawbacks which bear upon his neighbours. If the ground cannot be made to fit the system of allotment, the system must conform itself to the ground.

He then deals with a second way of allotting land. 'If you want the holding to lie in one compact patch', he says,

> you will have to make a very complicated reckoning of all the many circumstances which influence husbandry, will have to find some numerical expression for fertility, accessibility, and the like.

This second method is the one that Shetlanders used when they created lasts of land. The curse of runrig was that men and women had to wander all over their townships to have access to their fragments of land, and disputes frequently broke out about this or that morsel. The creation of lasts of land didn't abolish runrig,[120] but at least

---

119. Paul Vinogradoff, *Villainage in England: essays in English mediaeval history*, Oxford 1892, p.235
120. This point is vital. Cf. the statement in a sheriff court case of 1779 (Shetland Archives, SC.12/6/1779/12/3) that 'The lands of Aithseter, like most other lands in the country, lye run-rig. Every half last, as its called, or nine merks, are however someway distinguished.' Planking was a method of keeping runrig under control by confining it, rather than abolishing runrig. In the 1770s William Balfour remarked ruefully, concerning the township of Brindister in Gulberwick, that 'it is proposed to have these runrigg lands divided, but in the method usual in the country, which is still runrig upon a larger scale' (Shetland Archives, Hay & Co. Papers: Rental of Shetland c.1774). Even in the 1880s a crofter in Ure in Eshaness could tell the Crofters Commission that his land there was 'squared, but is still runrig' (*Shetland News*, 9 November 1889). As late as 1996 Cissie Smith told me that land at Channerwick in her young days was 'planked aboot' rather than 'rig aboot'.

mitigated the difficulties. Following the division of a township into two (Culswick), four (Bigton), six (Broo and Scatness in Dunrossness) or even (in the fertile island of Papa Stour) 12 lasts of land, each situated next to a specific house, arable land was far more accessible to the person who tilled it.

Such divisions were the raison-d'être of the last of land. In the early 1630s, for instance, Laurence Sinclair of Broo in Shetland, and Andrew Bruce of Muness, entered into a contract to divide the large township of Broo in half. (Broo no longer exists, having been obliterated by sand-blowing in the late seventeenth century). One of the parties reneged on the agreement, and the case eventually came to the court of session in Edinburgh. The lords made their decision in 1632.[121] They decreed that there should be a just and equal apportionment and division of the lands of Broo, 'ather', as they put it, 'be plankes, lastes or half lasts, as the samyn lyes in infield and outfield land'. They proposed that the division should be effected by four honest men.

This relatively early reference shows us the way in which Shetlanders used lasts of land, or planks as they increasingly came to call them,[122] to divide their arable land. Unfortunately, there are no detailed accounts of such divisions, or plankings, prior to the eighteenth century. It is to later and more informative occasions that I now turn.

'Ancient knowing men'

Most of what I'm going to say in this section is about Cunningsburgh, a district in the South Mainland of Shetland. Cunningsburgh is bisected by a large burn, and the two resulting areas were called, and are still called, Nort and Sooth Cunningsburgh. Each district traditionally contained eight lasts of land.

On two occasions, in the 1720s, and later in the the 1780s and 1790s, both Nort and Sooth Cunningsburgh were the subject of major redivisions, which enable us to see how lasts of land were created and deconstructed (so to speak). In 1724, for instance, there had been various irritating encroachments on some landowners' estates in Nort Cunningsburgh. In other words, some people had disregarded the traditional boundaries of the eight lasts of land there, to the annoyance of the landlords and tenants. The aggrieved parties purchased a brieve of perambulation from chancery, and as a result 15 'ancient knowing men' were appointed to consider the matter.[123]

It's worth quoting from the record of the perambulation to show exactly how the ancient knowing men carried out their task. They

> dide plank the samen through the severaull touns forsaid where they dide lye, and that according to the goodness and badness of the said lands, and after just metting, meithing and measuring and lyning made thereupon for the future dide affix and sett up march stons betuixt each plank for dividing, clairing and redding the severall planks the one from the other, conform to the ancient order practist and custome observed in affixing and setting up of march stons in all points.

---

121. National Archives of Scotland, CS.7/458, folio 53.
122. For another early reference to 'planks or lasts' see Shetland Archives, SC.12/53/1, p.442 (Agreement between heritors of Scatness, 1699): 'in which lands it is manifest that there is tuentie tuo merk and an half merk land of the kings property, lyand in the severall divisions, planks or lasts'.
123. Shetland Archives, D.6/68/1.

What these ancient men did was regularise the boundaries of the old lasts or planks of Nort Cunningsburgh: Aith (3 lasts), Aithsetter (2 lasts), Blosta and Gord (1 last each) and Keoda and Bremer (making up one last). They did so by ensuring that each last of land had its proper quota of good and bad land, using amicable discussion, common-sense and science. Then they set up march-stones to make the boundaries of the lasts or planks crystal clear and well-known. They expressed a hope that these stones would be marches in all time coming, and that all other fraudulent stones would be removed.

This division of 1724 is suggestive, but not too informative. The ancient honest men were simply adjusting a few boundaries around lasts or planks which had been in existence previously, probably for a very long time indeed. But in 1780 the proprietors of Sooth Cunningsburgh embarked on a division which was far more radical and is more instructive. Half a dozen experienced plankers (as they styled themselves) began work on 3 February, and continued for a week and a half. They drew a detailed plan, which unfortunately hasn't survived; but someone (I'm pleased to say) registered their calculations and notes in the sheriff court books of Shetland.[124]

I have to say at the outset that by the 1780s the method of creating lasts had been modified from its original 'pure' form. By 1780 it certainly wasn't the case that a last of land routinely paid 12 'shillings' – a last – of produce in rent. The traditional statement that this or that mark of land paid rent of so many 'pennies' of rent had also ceased to have much meaning.[125] The purpose of redividing the lands of Sooth Cunningsburgh in 1780 had far more to do with taking into account the modern structure of settlement in the district, which was very different from the ancient layout. Sooth Cunningsburgh, like Nort Cunningsburgh, had traditionally contained eight lasts of land, attached to old 'houses' there: Claphoull, with two lasts, and Vestanore, Vadsgarth, Brind, Beolka, Mail and Burraness with one each. By 1780, however, as we would expect, the population of the district had expanded in various directions: towards Clivigert to the south, and into Voxter and Aness to the east. Thus the plankers styled Voxter 'Out of the Town' (a name still used by people at Mail today to refer to their Voxter neighbours).

The plankers designed a series of five new lasts, or planks as they called them,[126] to accommodate the new structure of settlement in Sooth Cunningsburgh. These planks were different from each other in size and different in quality and value. The plankers continued to regard Sooth Cunningsburgh as containing 144 marks of arable land. However, they recognised that these marks, originally considered to be equal in quality as well as quantity, were now very different from each other. So they proceeded to reflect the difference in their new division.

They did exactly as Paul Vinogradoff prescribed: 'If you want the holding to lie

---

124. See Appendix, pp.92-4, *infra*.
125. Thomas Bolt wrote in 1809: 'untill of late years this distinction of penny land was strictly keeped to, all dispositions and every conveyance of land, the numbers of merks and what penny land they were were always mentioned particularly. Of late years that distinction of penny lands is for the most part given up' (Shetland Archives, D.24/2/35: Answers by Thomas Bolt to Mr Nicolson's queries).
126. The plankers of Sooth Cunningsburgh only used the word 'lasts' once in their report. However, lasts are clearly what they had in mind. A few months earlier one of them had taken part in a similar division of Scatness in Dunrossness (Shetland Archives SC.12/53/5, folio 74: 'The attested placing of the marches betwixt the four great planks of Scatness by the plankers'). In the record of the Scatness division the words 'plank' (or 'great plank') and 'last' are used interchangeably.

Figure 7 The communal meadows of North Cunningsburgh on an August day in the 1920s, looking towards Voxter and Aness (photograph by Jack Rattar). Folk are starting to transport 'coles' of hay back home – their carts are just visible in the middle distance – where they will be built into 'desses'. *Copyright Shetland Museum*

in one compact patch you will have to make a very complicated reckoning of all the many circumstances which influence husbandry, will have to find some numerical expression for fertility, accessibility, and the like'. The basic building block used by the Shetland plankers was the sub-plank, which had a precise areal value: it comprised 1,600 square fathoms. First they assigned a given number of marks of land to the five main planks: 48 marks to Claphoull, for instance, 42 to Beolka, and so on. They gave fewer marks to the more recent settlements: 21 to Voxter and a mere 9 to Aness. Then they divided the marks into sub-planks: the better the land the fewer sub-planks. For instance, Aness had 4½ sub-planks per mark, while the fertile and most ancient arable land at Beolka had one.

They did all this by making deductions about 'all the many circumstances which influence husbandry', as Vinogradoff put it. Even the best land had its drawbacks. 'Beolka', said the plankers,

> is mostly infields and good grass and meadows; it all lys very compact and is easily laboured, but ... by being surrounded by other planks and the sea, it can never be made larger, and being in the best state of cultivation it can never be made better; yet it is a little liable to sandblowing.

In fact there had been so much sandblowing that the ancient township of Burraness had disappeared.[127]

Vestanore was poorer land, but, as the plankers said, it 'is safe from sea gust, it has the hill or commonty almost round it, and the sea with plenty of ware at their doors; it has more than its proportion of meadow ground, and all its grass ground is improveable.' The question of accessibility to hill and sea, specially mentioned by Vinogradoff, was a vital consideration for the plankers. For instance, they said that Voxter 'is far from the hill or commonty', with 'hardly a possibility of a road to the hill, even for peats'. Even so, Voxter had 'tolerable good grass'. Only the most modern settlement, the little holding at Aness, had little or nothing going for it. 'Aness', they reported,

> is much liable to sea gust, has little ware, and is two miles from the hill or commonty; it has no meadows, and near the half of all its grass grounds is next to useless and can neither be improved to grass or corn for want of soil.

When they had finished their deliberations, they apportioned the actual possessions of the local landholders among the new planks. The biggest landowner by far was John Bruce of Sumburgh, who had 118 of the 144 marks of land in Sooth Cunningsburgh. As a result he got the lion's share: 37 planks and 1,120 square fathoms. The other proprietors got a mere six planks and 1,294 fathoms, apportioned carefully amongst the five great planks according to the whereabouts of their or their tenants' houses.

This division of Sooth Cunningsburgh in 1780 was state-of-the-art. But there were simpler ways of doing things. During the division of Nort Cunningsburgh, several years later, there was deep discussion among the landowners about whether more or less traditional methods of division were desirable. Some revolutionaries wanted to divide the land so thoroughly that every landowner had his or her land in a compact parcel. But Arthur Nicolson of Lochend thought that such a scheme would be expensive and undesirable. Nicolson preferred a traditional solution, and his musings on the subject contain a concise description of the old method of dividing Shetland land in lasts.[128]

'Suppose', he wheedled,

> that instead of laying each heritors land in one spot, as proposed ... the whole 144 merks [of Nort Cunningsburgh] be measured and laid in eight equal lasts, with a proportion of meadow and grass ground, and where one heritor is not proprietor of a whole last that he join with some other to make up a last.–That the eight lasts shall be laid in 8 different lotts, the greatest heritor having the choice of the first draught, the next greatest heritor the second draught, and so on.–The heritors and udallers who shall join in maner foresaid to make up a last shall subdivide among themselves in the best way they can.–This will make the general division much easier and shorter, whereas if the dividers are obliged to go on in subdividing and setting off to each udaller his or her merk, ure or half ure as they would wish to have it, the division will take up a deal of time to little purpose.

I'm certain that this scheme of Nicolson's was the ancient way of making lasts.

---

127. The name is still remembered in the district, but is now restricted to the ness or promontory.
128. Shetland Archives, SC.12/6/1787/1/4.

Others were nostalgic about the past as well. In 1797, for instance, John Bruce of Sumburgh (son of the John Bruce of 1780) promoted a division of Fladabister, the northmost part of Cunningsburgh, a township containing 36 marks of land. During the process Bruce contemplated various modes of division, and came down in favour of a traditional division according to lasts of land, or rather (in this case) half-lasts. According to Bruce[129] no

> plan of division will afford more general satisfaction than by dividing the whole room first into four half lasts of land, laying quantity for quallity where necessary, by which the defenders [Malcolm, Laurence and William Halcrow, portioners in Fladabister] would have a half last to themselves, William Bruce of Simbister, the pursuer and Edward Halcrow one last, and Lochend, Mr Heddell, George and James Williamson the remaining half last; then the few subdivisions which would be necessary in some of the ½ lasts might easily be performed by the landmeasurer and the smaller heritors' proportions laid off to them after the major heritors had made choice of their half lasts, either by lott, or the greatest proprietor to have the first choice and so on, as may be condescended on.

A quarter of a century later there was another division at Fladabister, and Bruce was still as keen as ever to promote his half-lasts. He entered a paper in the process[130] whose fifth point was

> That the whole room ... shall be divided into four principle divisions, consisting each of a half last, or nine merks of land, placing quantity for quality where it shall be found necessary. That as such a division will afford every requisite convenience to the proprietors, as well as it will facilitate the agricultural improvement of the place, as much as can be expected from any more extended division. No subdivision of the aforesaid half last of land shall take place, but at the exclusive expense of those who shall make choice of them.

The message from all this evidence is clear. Several landowners, amidst all the social and demographic change in Shetland at the turn of the nineteenth century, still regarded the last of land, or the half-last, as an efficient and inexpensive division tool. It moderated the inconvenience of runrig without involving the complexity and huge expenditure of a division according to proprietorship.

Whole township runrig

Why are there no lasts of land in Shetland today, and no vestige of them in place-names or (apparently) in the landscape? It's because of the social and demographic change I mentioned a moment ago. Runrig eventually proliferated until it was beyond the wit of the Shetlanders to keep it under control. Try as they did to mitigate its evil effects, the surge in population in the islands after 1770 meant that runrig burst the boundaries of the lasts of land. Everybody wanted her or his share of the best land in the township, and uncontrollable runrig was the result.[131] To give one example: it seems clear that in 1770 the township of Funzie in the island of Fetlar had a well-defined internal structure of 'houses' or lasts; by 1820, however, Funzie was a maze of runrig, with not the slightest trace of such an internal structure

---

129. Shetland Archives, SC.12/6/1797/53.
130. Shetland Archives, SC.12/6/1825/8.
131. For an unexpected linguistic result of runrig splitting see the 'Note on toonmels', pp.32-3, *infra*.

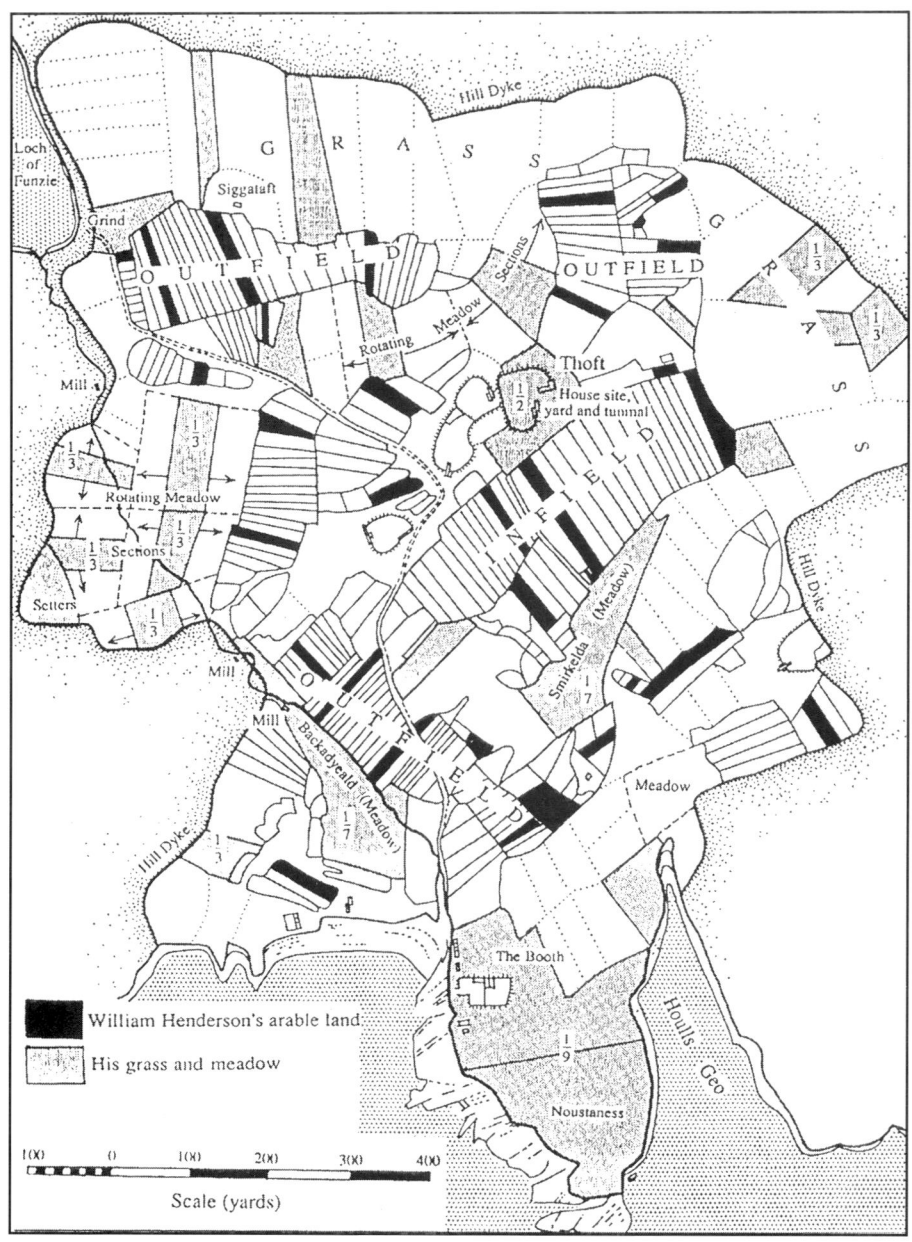

Figure 8 'Whole township' runrig at Funzie, Fetlar, in the 1820s, based on a plan by Andrew D. Mathewson. Funzie comprised about 72 marks of land. The plan shows the proliferating runrig, and the different categories of land (infield, outfield, grass and meadow) rented by one tenant, William Henderson. *Copyright W.P.L. Thomson.*

(see Figure 8). Willie Thomson calls this result 'whole-township runrig'.[132]

In the same way, the 12 lasts of land in Papa Stour disappeared, as runrig insinuated itself into every corner of the isle.[133] In 1849 Arthur Nicolson of Lochend, the main proprietor there, wrote to his solicitor to say that he had found an account of the 1724 division of Nort Cunningsburgh (see above, pp.25-6) among his papers. He compared the situation in Cunningsburgh in the 1720s with the current state of his property in Papa. 'In Cunningsburgh', he said perceptively, 'the principle was and is separation, in Papa diffusion as much as possible.'[134] In the middle ages, and right through to the eighteenth century, Papa had been one of the most fertile districts in Shetland; by 1849, with a population of nearly 500, it had become the most destitute.[135] The only way to deal with runrig in such a situation wasn't to keep it at arm's length, but to abolish it altogether – and that's what gradually happened throughout Shetland.

Division into lasts of land had been an ingenious idea. It was a local conception, thought up and elaborated by Shetlanders, and regulated by 'ancient knowing men'. While the population of the islands was small, division of townships into lasts or half-lasts kept runrig under control. Landowners were interested in the method, and closely supervised its operation, but they were content to let expert neutral Shetlanders deal with the details. As recently as 1914 the tenants of the little township of Williamsetter in Bigton reported to their landlord that one John Spence had just 'divided or planked' their land, 'according to a scheme suggested by ourselves', and that the result was satisfactory.[136]

Nowadays Shetlanders have never heard of lasts of land.[137] Sixteen years ago the late Freda Hutchison, who lived in Fladabister, wrote to me with her faint memories of the phrase.[138] 'Yes,' she said, 'my father and my mother too spoke about the eight last'. (She was talking about the eight lasts of land of Nort Cunningsburgh, which the ancient knowing men sorted out in 1724.) 'If anyone had gone for ... a visit of any kind, maybe even to the shop, and was a while in coming back, they would say, surely they are in the eight last this time.' But Freda didn't know what her parents meant by that statement. In AD 2000 Shetland is a land of villages surrounded by sheep. The dynamics and details of Shetland's ancient agricultural institutions have to be reconstructed from documents, because they have vanished forever from landscape and memory.

---

132. William P.L. Thomson, 'Township, house and tenant holding: the structure of run-rig agriculture in Shetland', in Val Turner ed., *The Shaping of Shetland*, Lerwick 1998, pp.107-27.
133. For a plan of the runrig of Papa Stour in 1846 see the endpapers of Barbara E. Crawford and Beverley Ballin Smith, *The Biggings, Papa Stour, Shetland: the history and excavation of a royal Norwegian farm*, Edinburgh 1999.
134. Shetland Archives, D.24, box 69, bundle of papers anent Papa division: Copy letter by Arthur Nicolson to Mr Sievwright, 22 May 1849.
135. Nicolson thought that Papa was 'the most destitute community in the islands' (National Archives of Scotland, HD.13/16: letter of 5 February 1849). I owe this reference to Jo Hanlon.
136. Shetland Archives, GD.144/156/6.
137. The word appears, but shouldn't, in John Graham, *The Shetland Dictionary*, Lerwick 1999, 'a picture of the Shetland speech as ... [the author has] known it during the middle decades of the twentieth century'.
138. Personal communication, 28 June 1984.

A note on toonmels

A 'toonmel' in Shetland today is the grass outside a house where the householder grazes her or his animals. The word often appears as a plural, for example 'her toonmels'. The word was also common in Orkney. Often spelled 'townmaill' in historical documents, there is no doubt about its etymology. A toonmel is Old Norse *tún völlr*, town field. When the lexicographer Jakob Jakobsen came to Shetland in the 1890s he found Shetlanders who pronounced it 'toonwel'.[139]

Toonmels were so called because they were the old arable core of a Shetland or Orkney township. In their modern stunted form they are the result of centuries of runrig husbandry. There are no detailed descriptions of Shetland townships from the seventeenth century, but a few accounts survive from that period in Orkney.[140] At that point Orkney toonmels weren't grass, but lovingly manured arable plots near the farmer's house, owned individually and not subject to runrig sharing. But as runrig marched on, it breached even those boundaries. By the nineteenth century the once prestigious arable toonmels had become scraps of grass. Of course, when new houses were built, both outside or inside a township's dykes, they needed toonmels as well. New toonmels, frequently unconnected with the old arable core of the township, were being created all the time.

A quarter of a century ago I thought that I understood toonmels, and runrig with its fissile processes. What I didn't bargain for was a series of revelations about the complex nomenclature of toonmels. One fine day in June 1976 I took a walk from my then home in Waas, on the Westside of Shetland, to Sandness. I stopped at Aggie and Gordon Walterson's house at Norby. They weren't in, and I sat down on their toonmel to wait.

When Aggie returned I referred, humorously, to my toonmel seat. She said: 'Does du ken whit a *tinmel* is?' Aggie comes from Fladabister, in the South Mainland of Shetland, and I assumed that 'tinmel' was a local pronunciation of toonmel there. She corrected me. A tinmel, she said, is a collection of farm- and office-houses in a township. Perplexed, I asked what she called the grass outside her door. 'Oh, we caa dat da *toons*,' she said.

Back in Waas I sought out my then landlord, John Jeromson of Greenland, and asked him what he called the grass outside his door. He thought for a moment, and said: 'Da toonloans'.

I brooded over these complexities for some time, and in December 1980 broadcast a little piece about the subject on Radio Shetland. I had consulted Jakobsen's *Etymological Dictionary* in the meantime, and found that he had recorded some of the variants. He had picked up 'tinmel' as well, and reckoned that it had precisely the same etymology as toonmel, despite the difference in meaning.

I had some response from my broadcast. Tom Tulloch of Gutcher wrote to tell me that in Nort Yell they spoke about 'da toonbøls' ('bøl' in Shetland dialect is an animal's resting-place). Tom Henderson, a native of Spiggie, at the opposite end of

---

139. Jakob Jakobsen, *An Etymological Dictionary of the Norn Language in Shetland*, London 1928-32 ('tunwel').
140. See J. Storer Clouston's fine account 'The Orkney townships', *Scottish Historical Review*, xvi, 1919, pp.16-45.

Figure 9 Collaquey, Northmavine, photographed by Robert Ramsay c.1890x1900. A cow is tethered on the toonmels. *Copyright Shetland Museum*

Shetland, reported that his folk spoke about 'da toonbøls' outside their door, but about the roof of a 'tinbøl'. George Gear of Lingness in South Nesting phoned to say that he and his neighbours spoke about 'da toonses'. Alan Fraser, at Crosbister in the Westing of Unst, told me that he remembered Unst folk speaking about 'da toombles': perhaps a variant of toonbøls, but markedly different in pronunciation. (Tulloch, Henderson, Gear, Fraser: great Shetland antiquaries, now gone.)

Gordon Walterson, not to be outdone by Aggie, recalled that in Sandness they spoke about 'da toons', over the hill in Dale of Waas 'da toonmels', and, next door to Dale, in Wast o Waas, 'da toonwins'. In addition, I noted that Jakobsen had found an instance of 'da toonens' – probably the same as toonwins – in Nort Roe; both of these, like Georgie's toonses, may be plurals of *tún*. And Willie Thomson, in his exemplary study of runrig at Funzie in Fetlar, had noted a toonmel called the 'toontig of Gardie': this time from Old Norse *teigr*, a strip of land.[141]

I have remained alert for new sightings. One day I heard Keetie Malcolmson, my aunt, speaking about a public eyesore. She said: 'For sicna tinmel!' Startled, I asked her to explain. She said that her mother, my grandmother, Andrina Mann of Da Blett in Sooth Cunningsburgh, had always used that phrase while scolding her children about untidiness. Robert Leask, a native of Bigton, then told me that when a crofter surrounded her house with proliferating henhouses and the like, her neighbours would say: 'She's gettin a proper tinmel yunder!'

It seemed that the further south in Shetland I went, there was a corresponding deterioration in the status of toonmels. My surmise was confirmed when I asked Ann Sinclair to make enquiries about the usage in Fair Isle. As in Cunningsburgh the Fair Islanders had no toonmels, but they had tinmels. In Fair Isle a tinmel, was not just a house, but a *ruined* house. Splitting in the townships had gone to such lengths that the phrase *tún völlr* had become attached to fragments of buildings!

---

141. William P.L. Thomson, 'Funzie, Fetlar: a Shetland runrig township in the nineteenth century'. *Scottish Geographical Magazine*, lxxxvi,1971, p.177.

The following four photographs (Figures 10-13) show toons of various sizes in the Mainland of Shetland, at different seasons in the 1930s. The first two photographs are by Jack Rattar; the others are by Lollie Scott. *All photographs courtesy of Shetland Museum.*

Figure 10 The first photograph is of Leveneep in Lunnasting, on 26 April 1939. Leveneep, an old scat-paying township, comprised 12 marks of land. Here we see it in 'voar', seed-time. The place has a relatively bleak aspect, now that winter stores of fodder have been used up, and before the new year's crops have started to grow. Most of the 'dess' – the haystack – is gone, because the animals have eaten it over the winter. Only one 'skroo' (corn stack) is left: over the winter the inhabitants have used the corn for themselves and for the animals.

Figure 11 The second photograph is of Da Forrats, an 'ootset' in Sandness, on a summer's day, looking towards the island of Papa Stour. Note how far this relatively modern ootset is from the ancient toons of Sandness at the shore. The first of the hay has been raked up into 'coles', and kail is still growing in the yard. The peats are home: the stacks are newly built and intact.

Figure 12 In the third photograph we see the toons at Wester Quarff. Neathaburn, in the foreground, comprised 18 marks of land; Upswall and Houll 15 marks; and Mews 18 marks: they are all ancient townships. It is a September day. Most of the grain crops have been cut and set up in 'stooks' on the rigs, and most of the hay has been cut and made into 'coles'. At the rig in the left foreground harvesting is in progress: corn is lying on the ground ready to be made up into sheaves. The sheep and cows are mostly out on the hill, but a few sheep are already in the toon, 'in krings': two together on one tether to stop them from straying onto crops. Once all the crops are in the yard the hill 'grinds' (gates) will be opened and the animals will be free to roam in the toons.

Figure 13 The final photograph is of Grunnavoe in Waas, another 12-mark scat-paying township, at a slightly later moment in the harvest. The corn 'stooks' have been gathered into bigger stacks called 'screevlings', and will eventually be taken into the yard to be built into a 'skroo'. There are potatoes in the rig on the left.

3

What is a scattald?

> [F]rom time immemorial the people have had the use of it, and it has been an understood thing that they were to have the scathold with the croft, because the crofts could not keep their families without the scathold.
> Do they consider they have a firmer right to this scathold than to the arable portion of the land? – Yes, they do, it appears that its name would imply that – a commonty for the common people.
> – George Sinclair, Shetland fish-curer and merchant, interrogated by Lord Napier in 1883 (*Parliamentary Papers* 1884, xxxiii, minutes of evidence, p.1344).

In 1884 Captain F.W.L. Thomas asked: 'What is a pennyland?'[142] By that date the pennylands of Orkney had ceased to have any social significance, and Thomas's investigation was very academic. A year previously Shetlanders had been asking and answering a similar question: 'What is a scattald?' The Shetland scattald or common was also an ancient institution, but the enquiry in Shetland, conducted by Lord Napier's crofting commission, wasn't so abstruse. During the six centuries covered by this essay the Shetland scattalds were a source of comfort and controversy to their inhabitants.

My concern here is with the functions and transformations of Shetland scattalds during the period from the fourteenth to the nineteenth centuries. I divide this period into two eras – from 1300 - 1750 and 1750 - 1900 – but as far as the scattald is concerned there wasn't a gulf between them. Enclosure came late in Shetland, and sometimes it didn't come at all. For 600 years scattalds were often living communities rather than private property.

Scatting

'Scattald' is a Shetland word. The opinion of lexicographers that it is common to Shetland and Orkney is wrong.[143] The etymology of the word is difficult. The first element is Old Norse *skattr*, tax, but the termination has puzzled scholars. Þorsteinn Vilhjálmsson has now made the brilliant suggestion that '-ald' in scattald is simply a noun-suffix of the kind attached to a few Old Norse roots, sometimes apparently to denote action and often related to appropriate verbs.[144] Examples are *farald*, journey, created from *fara*, to go, and *rekald*, a thing drifted ashore, from *reka*, to

---

142. See Introduction, *supra*, p.xi.
143. Thomas Edmondston, *Etymological Dictionary of the Shetland and Orkney Dialect*, Edinburgh 1866 ('scathald'); Jakob Jakobsen, *An Etymological Dictionary of the Norn Language in Shetland*, London 1928-32 ('skattald'); *Oxford English Dictionary* ('scattald'); *English Dialect Dictionary* ('scathold'); *Scottish National Dictionary* ('skatt'). The word 'scatles', cited by *Scottish National Dictionary* from an Orkney rental of c.1508, is 'scat-less', i.e. scat-free, not 'scattalds', as the original context makes clear (Alexander Peterkin, *Rentals of the Ancient Earldom and Bishoprick of Orkney*, Edinburgh 1820, section 1, p.85).
144. Personal communication, February 1996.

drift. If this is correct the verb in the background must be *skatta*, to impose tax; scattald might thus mean 'something [a place] scatted'.[145]

Figure 14 The hill dyke at Benigert, North Roe, photographed by Jack Peterson in 1949. The wall is built to have a pronounced tilt outwards, so that animals on the pasture were prevented from getting into the toon. If they did get in they could easily be driven out again. *Copyright Shetland Museum*

Scattalds were indeed scat-paying districts: they are twice called 'scatlands' in a document of 1577.[146] Our main source of information about them is a series of scat-books, taxation ledgers compiled by chamberlains of the 'Lordship' estate of Shetland. The most important are dated c.1510,[147] 1628[148] and 1716.[149] Each gives, in various states of completeness, a list of scat-paying districts in Shetland: about 200 single townships or groups of townships.

The two earliest scat-books refer to the districts in varying ways. Sometimes a single township pays scat on its own: 'Coultisuek'.[150] More often, however, we find townships grouped together: 'Kirkbust and Gryndescholl and Ham', or 'Calstay with the pertinence'.[151] On one or two occasions we find districts which aren't single townships at all: 'Konosbrocht', for instance.[152] The 1716 scat-book, compiled by Thomas Gifford of Busta, is far more detailed. The scat-paying districts have become 'scatalds': 'Twat scatald', 'Papall scatald', etc.[153] Gifford's book lists the

---

145. Ásgeir Blöndal Magnússon, *Íslensk Orðsifjabók*, Reykjavik 1989 (*'-ald'* and *'skatta'*). This method of word formation is still current in Iceland and Faroe: cf. mótald = modem (*Nøkur Teldorð*, Tórshavn 1990, p.10). I am grateful to Michael Barnes, Paul Bibire, Peter Foote and Jóhan Hendrik W. Poulsen for discussion of this matter. That such words were created in Shetland may be attested by the place-name Guttald in the island of Whalsay (HU 563613), a path for cattle and sheep, apparently from Old Norse *gata*, road. I owe this information to Ian Tait and John Jamieson.
146. John H. Ballantyne and Brian Smith eds., *Shetland Documents 1195-1579*, Lerwick 1999, pp.201-2.
147. John H. Ballantyne and Brian Smith eds., *Shetland Documents 1195-1579*, Lerwick 1999, Appendix 1.
148. National Archives of Scotland, E.41/7.
149. National Archives of Scotland, RH.9/15/176.
150. John H. Ballantyne and Brian Smith eds., *Shetland Documents 1195-1579*, Lerwick 1999, p.257.
151. John H. Ballantyne and Brian Smith eds., *Shetland Documents 1195-1579*, Lerwick 1999, pp.258, 259.
152. John H. Ballantyne and Brian Smith eds., *Shetland Documents 1195-1579*, Lerwick 1999, p.257.
153. National Archives of Scotland, RH.9/15/176, pp.45, 113

constituent townships of nearly every scattald in the islands, and it is possible for the first time to see the wide variations in size between the different districts. The island of Unst, for instance, contained the minute scattald of Kews, a single township, and also the scattald of Baliasta, incorporating nineteen.

In the sixteenth and the first half of the seventeenth century the scat-paying districts of Shetland paid 'lasts' of scat in cloth ('wadmal') and butter, exactly as their constituent townships paid 'lasts' of rent.[154] We saw in Chapter 1 that Papa Stour paid 12 'lasts' of rent: 1152 'pennies' of wadmal – 576 'pennies' of butter. That island also paid exactly one 'last' of scat: 96 'pennies' of wadmal + 48 'pennies' of butter.[155] It looks very much as if Shetland's rents and revenues were devised and imposed at the same time – perhaps the late thirteenth century – presumably by royal authority. That was certainly the arrangement in Norway, where land-rent and the tax *leidang* had a close relationship.[156]

It's likely, although there isn't a great deal of information on the subject, that the inhabitants of a scattald paid their scat collectively. The fact that the authors of the scat-books thought it sufficient to state the total scats payable by each area, rather than amounts due by individuals, may point to such a conclusion. In a list of payers of the tax wattle, dated 1605, 'Mairtein Dedistoun and his pertiners' are said to pay so much.[157] No doubt collective payment fell into disuse as time went on. In a note of scat and land-rent received in Shetland in 1652-3 most of the payments are credited to individuals, but there are still one or two references to payments by whole scattalds. For instance: 'scattill of Stenswale, receavit from the tenants per money, £11.9.0. Rests [i.e. owing by] Chene's aires 5s., which makis upe the scattill.'[158] And even in 1716 there are references to a few individuals who pay tax 'for him selfe and his nighbors'.[159]

Privileges

Some scholars have assumed, if only by using the spelling 'scathold', that a scattald was common grazing land 'held' in return for payment of scat or tax.[160] John Spence, a Shetland schoolteacher and antiquary, told Lord Napier in 1883 that[161]

> Shetland crofters have possessed the right of pasturage on the hills during a period of at least 900 years. Since the days of King Harold Harfagre of Norway, it has been held in lieu of a tax said to have been first imposed by him on the freeholders ... in the islands. ... This tax was called scat, hence the common is called scathold, or holding in lieu of scat.

---

154. See Chapter 2, *supra.*
155. National Archives of Scotland, E.41/7, folio 6.
156. See Magnus Lagabøter's Landlaw VII.7, where amounts of rent and tax are explicitly linked: R. Keyser and P.A. Munch eds, *Norges Gamle Love indtil 1387*, ii, Christiania 1845, p.108. This suggests that both types of payment were under central control, as Halvard Bjørkvik has proposed: 'Leidang', in *Kulturhistorisk Leksikon for Nordisk Middelalder*, x, Copenhagen 1981, col. 439.
157. National Archives of Scotland, E.41/7, folio 16: appendix to Rental of Yetland of c.1628.
158. Shetland Archives, GD.150/2015/B/1, folio 12.
159. National Archives of Scotland, RH.9/15/176, p.21.
160. This is the explanation favoured by Oxford English Dictionary, cited (with a caveat) by *Scottish National Dictionary* and *Dictionary of the Older Scottish Tongue.*
161. *Parliamentary Papers* 1884, xxxiii, minutes of evidence, p.1430.

Others, from Thomas onwards,[162] have worried away at an entirely different idea. They state that scat in Shetland was a payment for arable rather than grazing land, basing their argument on the fact that scat wasn't paid when land was ley. Alfred Johnston took up this theme again and again, notably in a discourteous editorial footnote to an article by Jessie Saxby. Saxby had said that the Shetlanders paid scat 'for the use of the commons – the daals and fiels and saiters where their animals fed and from whence they got their fuel'.[163] No, interjected Johnston,

> in accordance with the practice of the mother country, Norway, and of Orkney, skatt was a tax paid to the Government for the cultivated lands. There is absolutely no proof that the practice differed in Shetland.

The point is, however, that although scat was levied on arable land, it was nonetheless paid *for the use of* a bundle of privileges inside and outside the merely arable part of a township. Shetlanders paid rent according to the mark of land (see Chapter 1, *supra*), and scat in proportion, for access to arable, meadow and grazing land. The antiquarian Thomas Irvine put it well in 1868: 'A merk of land ... means arable, grass and meadow within dike and a merk's share of the skathold.'[164]

It was virtually impossible to live in Shetland without grazing land. As a result, the word 'scattald' became specially associated with pasture. A document of 1646 refers to 'muir, hill, scattell and friedome' as synonyms.[165] There were plenty of hills in Shetland: so many that overstocking rarely seems to have been a problem. As late as the 1840s, when the population of the islands was soaring, the minister of Sandsting said calmly that 'every tenant exercises an unlimited privilege of pasturage on the hills or scathold', with the result that 'no other person can possibly know the number of sheep belonging to each individual.'[166] The fact that grazing rights were eventually regarded as the main privilege in a scattald is shown by the use of the verb 'to scat', or even 'to scatle', to refer to the practice of townships grazing together in one place.[167] In 1738 the presbytery of Shetland asked various people in the parish of Tingwall: 'what priviledge you know Tingwall had of ... scatling of sheep in the hills?' Jacob Tait answered that he knew 'nothing further ... than that Tingwall and Walster scatt together.'[168] This unusual verb was long-lived. As late as 1894 a Shetland factor told a royal commission that 'John Harper and Agnes Moar are the names of these who have scattald, and they scat on the scattald outside the dyke and right to the dykes of Uyeasound'.[169]

---

162. F.W.L. Thomas, 'What is a pennyland? or ancient valuation of land in the Scottish Isles', *Proceedings of the Society of Antiquaries of Scotland*, new series, vi, 1884, p.279.
163. Jessie M.E. Saxby, 'Shetland phrase and idiom, ii', *Old Lore Miscellany*, i, 1907-8, pp.268-9.
164. Shetland Archives, D.16/392/2/7: Letter by Thomas Irvine to Messrs Sievwright, 13 November 1868.
165. National Archives of Scotland, RS.44/4, folio 303: Instrument of sasine in favour of William Bruce, following feu charter by William Bruce of Soundbrugh, 21 May 1646. I am grateful to Jennifer Perry for assistance with this reference.
166. John Bryden, 'United parishes of Sandsting and Aithsting', *The Statistical Account of the Shetland Islands*, Edinburgh and London 1841, p.126. A fishcurer told Lord Napier in 1883: 'I don't know if any person could really tell the number of square miles of commonty here, and any person can keep as much stock as they like and can attend to' (*Parliamentary Papers* 1884, xxxiii, minutes of evidence, p.1340).
167. Jakob Jakobsen regarded this use of the verb as late: *An Etymological Dictionary of the Norn Language in Shetland*, London 1928-32 ('skatt').
168. Shetland Archives, CH.2/1071/3, pp.202, 204.
169. *Parliamentary Papers* 1895, xxxix, part 1, minutes of evidence, p.1118.

Figure 15 Cattle on hill pasture near Tumblin, Aithsting, on a summer day in the 1920s (photographer Jack Rattar). *Copyright Shetland Museum*

Although communal grazing was an important activity in a scattald there were others, depending on the natural endowments of the district. There could be 'liberty to strike thack, cast feals or peats, etc.'[170] According to a list of the scattald marches of Unst, drawn up in 1771, 'all lands that pay scatt draw their proportional shares of tang, sea-ware or weed, raga or driven wood, whales and wrecks within their respective boundaries'.[171]

A clear picture of the way these arrangements were made in practice emerges from two documents dated 1431 and 1681. The first describes a visitation by neighbours – a 'hagrie', as it was known in Shetland – to beat the bounds of a scat-paying district.[172] The district comprised the townships of Caldback, Gert and Crookster in Delting, now obliterated by oil installations. They are said to have various (slightly different) privileges in the surrounding hills and shores 'effter skattom senom', or 'efftir thair skat', as the copyist renders it in an impromptu translation. These privileges mainly concerned grazing, but included rights to cut 'tang' ('wair eb' or seaweed), and to collect 'vade oc raka' ('dryffin tymmyr and waiding').[173] The word 'scattald' doesn't appear in the document, but the three townships together clearly make up what was later known as a scattald. They duly appear together as 'Garth scatald' in Gifford's 1716 scat-book.[174]

There is similar information in a 'haggrie of Esharess', written down a quarter of

---

170. Shetland Archives, CH.2/151/14/5: Extract from book of marches and scattalds of Fetlar, 1710.
171. Alfred W. Johnston, 'Scattald marches of Unst in 1771', *Old-lore Miscellany of the Viking Club*, iii, 1910, p.101.
172. John H. Ballantyne and Brian Smith eds., *Shetland Documents 1195-1579*, Lerwick 1999, no. 21.
173. See the 'Note on Waithing and waith', pp.58-63, *infra*.
174. National Archives of Scotland, RH.9/15/176, p.69.

a millennium later.[175] Here we find in even more detail the way in which different townships within a single scattald had specific grazing rights, privileges in parts of the seashore, and even offshore islands. For instance,

> Trumblesgow [a creek] belongs to [the townships of] Framgord and Garderhouse. ... The holm of Fuglaskerrie belongeth one year to Framgord and one to Breckon and Garderhouse.

But the system of rights and privileges was more complicated than even these documents reveal. An inhabitant of a scattald could just as easily find herself *excluded* from privileges. People who didn't pay scat, because they lived in an 'ootset' which wasn't ancient enough to have been scatted, didn't have an automatic right to participate in the scattald's benefits. Thus, 'the room of Gardon [in Unst] pays no scatt and has no priviledge without its dykes'.[176] In the same way, as William Balfour wrote c.1774, 'small islands, though inhabited from early times, if they have no right of commonage upon the mainland or next adjacent large island, pay no scatt'.[177] Those excluded in this way had to pay 'hogaleaves'[178] to get access to grazing: Gardon, for instance, had 'peats and thatch from Snabrough, for which they pay a yearly payment called hogaleave'.[179] Hence the terms 'scattilmen',[180] 'scat brethren',[181] 'scatlers',[182] and 'inscatlders', to refer to people with scattald rights, and 'utscatlders' to denote those excluded.[183]

'He wished he might be struck blind if this was not the march'

'A uniform concern of all regulations is to exclude interlopers from outside the parish from using the common. This is as old as regulation itself.'[184] Shetland's laws protected neighbours in a scattald from trespassers. In 1602 Magnus Daile rode someone's mare 'without leave, over four scattellis of land'; Earl Patrick Stewart fined him forty shillings per scattald.[185] In the same way, it was unlawful

> to ony persone or persones at ony tyme of day, bot especiallie afoir the sune rysing and efter the soone setting, to go throuch his nychtbouris scattell or comontie with ane scheip dog, except he be accompanyed with ane or twa nychtbouris, famous honest men.[186]

---

175. Shetland Archives, SA.2/178.
176. Alfred W. Johnston, 'Scattald marches of Unst in 1771', *Old-lore Miscellany of the Viking Club*, iii, 1910, p.217.
177. Shetland Archives, Hay & Co. Papers: Rental of Shetland c.1774.
178. Jakob Jakobsen, *An Etymological Dictionary of the Norn Language in Shetland*, London 1928-32 ('hogalif').
179. Alfred W. Johnston, 'Scattald marches of Unst in 1771', *Old-lore Miscellany of the Viking Club*, iii, 1910, p.217.
180. Gordon Donaldson ed., *The Court Book of Shetland 1602-1604*, Edinburgh 1954, p.248.
181. Shetland Archives, Hay & Co. Papers: Rental of Shetland c.1774.
182. Shetland Archives, D.25/62/1: Petition by Thomas Lauranson in South Caldclift, 'with all the other scatlers', c.July 1762, to sheriff depute, anent abuse of hill of Hadreslie by swine. For a reference of 1667 to 'the scattellers of Strand and Nebeback' in Yell see appendix p.88, *infra*.
183. Thomas Gifford, *An Historical Description of the Zetland Islands*, [London 1786], Sandwick 1976, p.84, where the words are misspelled 'inscalders' and 'ulscalders'. As early as the 1570s we find two references to 'the inscattell callit infeild or outscattell callit outfeild' (John H. Ballantyne and Brian Smith eds., *Shetland Documents 1195-1579*, nos. 221 and 236).
184. E.P. Thompson, *Customs in Common*, London 1991, p.147.
185. Gordon Donaldson ed., *The Court Book of Shetland 1602-1604*, Edinburgh 1954, p.34: see also pp.88, 133.
186. Gordon Donaldson ed., *The Court Book of Shetland 1615-1629*, Lerwick 1991, pp.160-1.

Figure 16 John Smith closes the hill grind at Wadbister, Bressay, c.1900 (photographer James Smith). *Copyright Shetland Museum*

To control access to their privileges Shetlanders memorised their scattald boundaries with great care. Usually the details were too well known to be written down, and it is a surprise to find an account of the boundaries of Symbister scattald in a charter of 1608.[187] They began 'on the north syd of the erable landis of Simbister', and passed

> to the sey dyk of Seter, from thair estward to the north dyk of Lewesetter, and from thair eastward to the loche of Hoxsetter, and sua as the loche fallis in the sey; frome thyne sowthwestward to the dyk of Clet and Sandwick, and from Sandwick to the lockeit ness of Simbister, and from thyne to the gairdie callit Hamneseter.

I have already mentioned the 'hagrie' (Old Norse *haga-reið,* 'pasture-ride'), the ceremony of establishing the boundaries of a scattald. Hagries were great occasions, when the 'honestest' men of the parish perambulated the scattald marches together.[188] During the perambulations the adults beat youngsters, to imprint the marches on their memories, and there is a reference to such an assault in a document dated 1843:[189]

---

187. John H. Ballantyne and Brian Smith eds., *Shetland Documents 1580-1611*, Lerwick 1994, no. 442.
188. Gordon Donaldson ed., *The Court Book of Shetland 1615-1629*, Lerwick 1991, p.167.
189. Shetland Archives, D.16/389/25/1.

at a perambulation of the scattald marches of Unst in the year 1818 or 1819 ... Mr Mowat to make it to be the better remembred that Tonga was the march, gave Fredman Stickle, one of the parties present ... a crack over the back with his horse-whip.

Sometimes there was consolation for the bairns. In 1829 Laurence Jamieson, a tenant in Channerwick, recalled how, years previously,[190]

the Channerwick people took a little lassie to the spot to witness the placing of the stone, and gave her three scelps upon her loare, by which he understands her hip, and for which she received a shilling.

Hagries seem to have gone out of use in the mid-eighteenth century, after the abolition of heritable jurisdictions in 1747.[191] At that moment Shetland's bailie-courts, which organised the hagries, and oversaw Shetland's 'Country Acts', a code of local agricultural legislation, fell into disuse. But Shetlanders continued to memorise their scattald boundaries with care. At a legal enquiry in Fetlar in 1888 several old people could repeat a jingle for the benefit of the court:[192]

Kettle-o'-Stane, Staney Lee, Skipta-Skerry in the sea,
Marks the scattald of Tresta, Toun and Velzie.

All in all, the certification of scattald boundaries was a serious business. During an investigation of marches in the hills near Sandwick in the 1820s or 1830s, one Laurence Halcrow dug up a rock, to establish whether or not there were whelks underneath (a common method of identifying real march-stones). 'Laurence ... said he wished he might be struck blind if this was not the march.' It wasn't – and 'very shortly after he was struck blind and remained blind till his death.'[193]

Once interlopers had been excluded, scattalds became 'neighbourhoods'. For Gilbert Goudie, writing at the very end of our period,[194]

so clearly is the Skathald identified with the very life of the people that frequently a whole district is known and denominated by the Skathald to which the occupants have right in common–e.g. 'the Skathald of ...' ... in place of designing the residents by the townships which are contained in the district.

The idea of the scattald as a neighbourhood unit was built into the legal arrangements of the islands. As well as grazing animals, cutting peats and collecting driftwood together, the 'nichtbouris that duellis [dwells] within ane scathald' were expected to acquit (or refuse to acquit) each other of crimes committed there.[195] And if one person in the scattald acted in an anti-social way the

---

190. Shetland Archives, SC 12/6/1826/40a. Laurence got it slightly wrong: the lassie's 'loare' was her thigh (Old Norse *lær*). John Turnbull also reports that children employed in this way 'received some little reward' ('United parishes of Tingwall, Whiteness and Weesdale', *The Statistical Account of the Shetland Islands*, Edinburgh and London 1841, p.64).
191. According to William Balfour 'it was solemnised in one or two parishes in or about the year 1745' (Shetland Archives, Hay & Co. Papers: Rental of Shetland c.1774).
192. *Shetland News*, 4 August 1888. There was consternation in Fetlar in 1999 when Kettle-o'-Stane went missing. It turned out that the Shetland Bird Club had borrowed it to make a memorial for a well-loved local ornithologist. I am grateful to John Coutts for this information.
193. Shetland Archives, D.8/418/12: statement anent scattald boundaries, 19 May 1874.
194. *Scottish Leader*, 5 November 1889.
195. John H. Ballantyne and Brian Smith eds., *Shetland Documents 1195-1579*, Lerwick 1999, p.203.

whole scattald might be fined. When Bruce of Cultmalindie tried to fine individuals instead in the 1570s there was outcry:[196]

> for breiking of nichtbourheid, the haill ... scattale payit fyve gudlingis; now he compellit ilk man in the parochin to pay for the said unlaw fyve gudlingis, quhilk will extend to grit sowmes, to the grit hurt of us the inhabitantis of the cuntrie.

Because the scattald was the site for so much communal activity, some scholars have assumed that it was a very ancient institution: 'coeval with the settlement of the first Norwegian colonists',[197] according to one; pre-Norse in origin in the view of others.[198] None of these scenarios is at all likely. My tentative suggestion is that the scat-paying districts in Shetland may have reached their relatively final form in the thirteenth century, when (as I have argued[199]) scat and rent began to be levied on districts and townships in Shetland. This process must have created well-defined territorial units, and must gradually have replaced shifting spheres of interest controlled by individuals.

In due course these units comprised unscatted as well as scatted townships. In the thirteenth century, for instance, the island of Papa Stour contained at least one township that 'wasn't rented out as part of the "scat land"' of the main settlement there (according to one of the parties in an argument).[200] As time passed the boundaries between the districts became more and more firmly established. Scattalds, with their communal responsibilities and privileges, became the basic settlement districts of the islands.

'The great support of the inhabitants'

During the eighteenth and nineteenth centuries common land in Scotland virtually disappeared. In Shetland, however, a very different series of events took place.

As is well known, the economy and society of Shetland was transformed during the eighteenth century: within the space of a generation or two everyone in Shetland became part of a huge commercial fishing concern.[201] But the change was more dramatic offshore than it was on the land. Under the new regime the people who caught the fish, and the merchant-lairds who bought them, had no desire to enclose the scattalds or abolish their privileges. Landlords sought to attract and conciliate fishing tenants by providing small farms and extensive pastures for them.

William Balfour's report on the 'Lordship' estate of Shetland, compiled in the 1770s, is full of remarks to that effect. Outer Skaw in Unst, he wrote, 'is a good

---

196. John H. Ballantyne and Brian Smith eds., *Shetland Documents 1195-1579*, Lerwick 1999, p.203.
197. Laurence Edmondston, 'General observations on the county of Shetland', *The Statistical Account of the Shetland Islands*, Edinburgh and London 1841, p.168.
198. Including your author. In the original version of this essay I made the barmy statement that the territorial units of Iron Age Dunrossness were almost identical to the seventeenth century scattalds of that parish. In fact we know nothing at all about the prehistoric territories and communities of Shetland: the modalities of settlement or the relations of production of the people who lived here. There have been even wilder claims about the Orkney settlement districts. Colin Renfrew has cited with approval a notion that 'the distribution of medieval chapels in Orkney, which is itself related to the Norse system of rental districts, may show a continuity with the preceding Pictish tenurial system, and may indeed extend back to the first millennium B.C.' (Colin Renfrew ed., *The Prehistory of Orkney*, Edinburgh 1985, p.248). But for more reasoned discussion of such themes see V. Gordon Childe, 'Note on the chambered cairns of Rousay', *Antiquaries Journal*, xxii, 1942, pp.139-41.
199. See Chapter 1, *supra*.
200. See Chapter 1, *supra*.
201. See Chapter 4, *infra*.

fishing situation, the scatald large and peats near'. 'The scatald of this town', he wrote about Strand in Fetlar, 'compared with others in the neighbourhood, is not of great extent, but before it was so very much peeled, was unquestionably the finest sheep pasture in Shetland'. But he had no plans to enclose it. When tenants on adjacent estates encroached on his tenants' scattald rights Balfour immediately voiced his concern. At Stromfirth he found that [202]

> the scatald is confined, and the possession ... disputed ... by the possessors of Catfirth in the parish of Nesting, a dispute of which the grounds ought to be inquired into, as the scatalds where they are extensive and commodious are the great support of the inhabitants.

Far from being ripe for 'improvement', then, the Shetland scattalds were popular with everyone. As in previous centuries the law courts did their bit to protect them. In 1725 Thomas Gifford, stewart and justiciar depute of the islands, a prosperous fish-merchant, re-enunciated the 'Country Acts', with their rules about use of scattalds, as a useful mainstay of the new fishing tenure system,[203] and during the following century his successors did so again and again. In 1790 the Commissioners of Supply of Shetland decided[204] that the Acts were

> of a salutary nature, and have been observed for more than a century back, and ought still to be observed unless where a particular law of a more recent date shall be thought by the judge ordinary directly inconsistent with them.

They sent a copy of them to every minister in the islands, 'respecting as a favour done to the country that they will cause them to be read by their clerk once a year at least upon some lawful day appointed by the minister for that purpose'. One Shetland landowner was invoking that 'set of wholesome local regulations, called the "Country Acts of Zetland"' as late as 1836.[205]

But some changes, if only in pace, were inevitable. As the population of Shetland rose dramatically during the eighteenth century there was growing pressure on the scattalds and the resources they provided for the fishing economy. In 1756 the minister of Dunrossness complained that the laird of Quendale had 'set in tennants' on the scattald of Skelberry, part of which was the glebe, 'without so much as asking the concurrence of the minister, as usual in such cases'.[206] The laird was of course creating accommodation for his fishing tenants, and despite the minister's complaint this movement to establish 'ootsets' on the scattalds was irreversible. In about 1770 it was estimated that there were already about 380 of them.[207]

Inevitable or not, attempts to establish ootsets, which were in effect small enclosures, were resented by the Shetlanders. In 1785 John Bruce of Sumburgh directed two of his tenants on the island of Mousa to break out new holdings at a spot called the Blett in the scattald of Sooth Cunningsburgh.[208] As a result various small

---

202. Shetland Archives, Hay & Co. Papers: Rental of Shetland c.1774.
203. Thomas Gifford, *An Historical Description of the Zetland Islands* [1786], Sandwick 1976, pp.89ff.
204. Shetland Archives, SC.12/53/6, folio 168.
205. Gilbert Goudie, *Antiquities of Shetland,* Edinburgh and London 1904, p.244.
206. Shetland Archives, CH.2/1071/4, p.197.
207. Shetland Archives, SA.2/53.
208. Shetland Archives, SC 12/6/1787/1. One of the tenants was your author's great-great-great grandfather.

landowners and tenants there

> did in a tumultious manner ... enter the inclosure of the Blett, with spaids and other instruments of agriculture, and without any rule or rhime or reason, each heritor and heritors tenants apropriated such a peice of the said grounds ... to his own use.

Incidents like these didn't signal the last gasp of threatened communities, but are rather proof of the continued vitality of Shetland's rural communities. Certainly, the merchant lairds of Shetland were busily snapping up arable land throughout the islands, and dispossessing small proprietors where they could. But their main purpose in doing so was to amass fishing tenants. By leaving the scattalds virtually unenclosed, and devoting their energies to the maritime part of their estates, they gave the Shetlanders a breathing space.

Strangers, especially those from Scotland, were bemused by the political economy of Shetland, not least by the scattalds. Sir Walter Scott, visiting Shetland in 1814, wrote in his diary[209] that he was unable to

> get a distinct account of the land rights. The udal proprietors have ceased to exist, yet proper feudal tenures seem ill understood. Districts of ground are in many instances understood to belong to townships or communities, possessing what may be arable by patches and what is muir by commonty pro indiviso.

In other words, the old scattald system, still alive and kicking.

Mania

Divisions of scattald were indeed in the offing. The first successful division in Shetland according to the 1695 Act of Division of Commonty was that of the scattald of Fitful Head in Dunrossness, raised in 1815 and completed in 1826.[210] Fifty years later it was possible for someone to write that 'nearly all the scattald marches in Shetland have been judicially fixed, and the scattalds divided among the respective proprietors'.[211] But we must ask: how significant was this movement in reshaping rural communities in Shetland? By the 1820s Shetland landlords had more or less dropped out of the fishing trade. In future they would lease their estates and fishing tenants to merchants instead.[212] They now began to turn their attention to their overgrazed and chaotically-managed estates, and concluded that to make things more efficient they should separate their tenants' grazing land from that of adjacent proprietors. But division *in itself* didn't create havoc in Shetland society. As Lord Napier mused in 1883, if a division took place, and a proprietor 'got his own share ... and left it in the occupation of his own crofters, they would not say that he had taken away their land, would they?'[213]

No: the important rural movement in nineteenth century Shetland wasn't the division of the scattalds, but the enclosure of scattalds and some arable land for use as sheep-farms. This major mutation in the social history of Shetland has been

---

209. Walter Scott, *Northern Lights*, Hawick 1982, p.29
210. Susan Knox, *The Making of the Shetland Landscape*, Edinburgh 1985, pp.365-6.
211. Shetland Archives, GD.144/211/24.
212. See Chapter 4, *infra*.
213. *Parliamentary Papers* 1884, xxxiii, minutes of evidence, p.1408.

largely ignored by historians. The point about scattald confiscations and clearances was that they were the antithesis of the fishing tenure system, and their proponents and opponents saw them in precisely that way.

The first theorist of Shetland sheep farms was Arthur Nicolson of Lochend, the laird of Fetlar. On 3 January 1826 he wrote an extraordinary letter to the 'young men' of the island, in which he set out his terms for the continued existence of the population there.[214] He noted with disapproval that 'the whole male population of the island have betaken themselves to the trade of English sailors '– *i.e.* the Greenland whaling, a favourite escape route from fishing tenure – with the result that 'in a few years ... not a man in the island would be able to act the part either of a farmer or fisherman'. (It was a ludicrous analysis.) He therefore gave the young men an ultimatum: stay at home and fish for him or merchants chosen by him, or face eviction to accommodate sheep, and thus 'triple the income of the proprietors'. The young men apparently called Nicolson's bluff, and he did what he had threatened. Before his death in 1863 he had cleared most of the West Isle of Fetlar, and built dykes to enclose the scattalds. 'In thirty years 300 people – mostly the young active men and women – had had to find homes outwith the island.'[215]

The sheep-farms of nineteenth century Shetland appeared in two main phases (see Figure 18). The first clearances took place in Fetlar, Weisdale and Tingwall, from the 1820s to the 1850s.[216] Catastrophic as these were for the evicted and deprived tenants, public opinion in Shetland was muted. In 1855 an anonymous Shetland correspondent, speaking about the Weisdale clearances, remarked that 'the exterminating process of improvement ... may have some admirers in Shetland, but they are very few'.[217] But there was little open comment, let alone resistance. Most of the early clearances took place in the central area of Shetland, and didn't interfere with the fishing tenure system, which was mainly based in the periphery.

The second phase was another matter. The background to it was the development of better communications with the mainland of Scotland, which enabled the new farmers to export large numbers of sheep.[218] From about 1867 sheep-farming in Shetland became a 'mania'.[219] A glance at Figure 18 will show the number and extent of the scattald confiscations and croft clearances involved. At the same time, public comment on the sheep farms, both by their owners and opponents, was far fiercer than it had been in the first phase.

The main protagonist for the new policy was John Walker (see Figure 17), a native of Aberdeen who had prospected for gold in Australia, and had arrived in Shetland about 1860.[220] He immediately set out to become the scourge of the Shetland landlords and merchants who ran the fishing tenure system, which, he reckoned, made the Shetlanders hopelessly improvident. 'When I went there a few

---

214. Shetland Archives, D.6/176/1.2
215. Robert L. Johnson, 'The deserted homesteads of Fetlar', *Shetland Life*, no. 13, 1981, p.35.
216. See Figure 18 for details and sources.
217. *Northern Ensign,* 17 July 1856.
218. H. Evershed, 'On the agriculture of the islands of Shetland', *Transactions of the Highland and Agricultural Society of Scotland,* 4th series, vi, 1874, p.187n.
219. *Shetland Times,* 27 October 1888 editorial.
220. I am grateful to Susan Cooper, Wendy Gear and Jane Manson for much discussion and information about John Walker.

years ago ...' he said in 1871, 'I saw ... that the commons were of no use to the people, and were doing them harm. I at once resolved to take the commons from them.'[221] With the assistance of Major Cameron, a prominent Shetland laird, he confiscated huge expanses of scattald in Delting and Yell. David Charles Edmondston, an Unst laird, followed his example. The reaction in Shetland was violent. The tenants, said Walker, 'were so shocked ... that for a time they were to practise a little shooting at me on the point. ... I did carry a revolver for a month, but I had no occasion to use it'.[222]

Figure 17 John Walker (1835-1916) and his wife Mary Plummer, in Australia in the 1850s, a few years before they came to Shetland. *Copyright Shetland Museum*

This is not to acquit Shetland's landlords from responsibility. Many of them were implicated in the sheep-farm movement – not least because the farmers had to lease their farms from them. This didn't prevent some landlords from remaining interested in fishing tenure as well: consider the case of John Bruce of Sumburgh, who ran a huge sheep farm in Cunningsburgh, but simultaneously forced his Dunrossness tenants to fish for him.[223]

Perhaps the most interesting case of dual interests is that displayed by several merchants in Unst who forestalled John Walker in an attempt to confiscate the

---

221. *Parliamentary Papers* 1871, xxxvi, minutes of evidence, p.886. Walker returned to the same theme a year later: 'You must bear in mind that I don't think it is for the interests of the working people in Shetland to have scattald' (*Parliamentary Papers* 1872, xxxv, minutes of evidence, p.405).
222. *Parliamentary Papers* 1871, xxxvi, minutes of evidence, p.886.
223. *Parliamentary Papers* 1872, xxxv, minutes of evidence, pp.329f.

Major croft clearances and scattald confiscations in Shetland, c.1820-c.1875

The map refers to only 14 examples of croft clearance and scattald confiscation. There were many others, as can be seen from the Book of Reference and maps appended to the Deer Forest Commission report, which list 69 proposed restitutions of pasture (*Parliamentary Papers* 1895, xxxviii, appendix, pp.60-5). Nor is it meant to suggest that no confiscations of scattald took place *after* 1875: cf. the confiscation of the scattalds of Skelberry in Dunrossness in 1886 (*Shetland Times*, 31 August 1889) and Virdifield in c.1890 (*Parliamentary Papers* 1895, xxxix, part 1, minutes of evidence, pp.1108-9).

1. Burrafirth and Cliff, Buness estate, Unst. Cleared in late 1860s and made into a 1,500-acre sheep farm (H. Evershed, 'On the agriculture of the islands of Shetland', *Transactions of the Highland and Agricultural Society of Scotland*, 4th series, vi, 1874, pp.214-15).
2. Ordale, Buness estate, Unst. Cleared in late 1860s and made into a 2,000-acre sheep farm (Evershed, 'On the agriculture', pp.214-5).
3. Rue, Buness estate, Unst. Cleared c.1872 and made into a sheep farm (*Parliamentary Papers* 1884, xxxiii, minutes of evidence, pp.1291-5). 99 acres old arable and 695 pasture scheduled by Deer Forest Commission.
4. North Yell, Garth estate. Many crofts cleared in late 1860s and incorporated in five sheep farms, comprising nearly 10,000 acres (R. Scot-Skirving, 'On the agriculture of the islands of Shetland', *Transactions of the Highland and Agricultural Society of Scotland*, 4th series, vi, 1874, p.261; *Parliamentary Papers* 1884, xxxiii, minutes of evidence, pp.1278-81, 1284-5).
5. Windhouse, Garth estate, Mid Yell. Cleared in late 1860s and made into a 3,000-acre sheep farm (Scot Skirving, 'On the agriculture', p.261).
6. Fetlar, Nicolson estate. Whole West Isle and Lambhoga peninsula cleared c.1820-60 (Robert L. Johnson, 'The deserted homesteads of Fetlar', *Shetland Life*, no. 13, 1981, pp.26-35). 389 acres old arable and 2,989 pasture scheduled by Deer Forest Commission.
7. Tingon, Cheyne estate. About 14 families evicted in 1865 (*Edinburgh Evening Courant*, June 1865; personal communication by Bruce Benson, author of a forthcoming paper on this clearance).
8. North Delting, Garth estate. Extensive scattald and croft clearances in late 1860s, resulting in 2,500-acre sheep farm (Scot Skirving, 'On the agriculture', p.259).
9. Lunnasting, Bell estate. Extensive scattald confiscations over a long period (*Shetland Times*, 28 September and 5 October 1889). 57 acres old arable and 1,035 acres pasture scheduled by Deer Forest Commission.
10. Whalsay, Symbister estate. Much of scattald confiscated 1865, and made into a 1,300-acre sheep farm (Evershed, 'On the agriculture', p.215; Scot Skirving, 'On the agriculture', p.259).
11. Weisdale, Black estate. Extensive clearances c.1850 (John Graham, 'The Weisdale evictions', *New Shetlander*, no. 130, pp.29-31). 228 acres old arable and 4,018 acres pasture scheduled by Deer Forest Commission.
12. Veensgarth and Dale, Hayfield estate, Tingwall. Cleared in 1850s-60s, and made into a 4,000 acre sheep farm (William P.L. Thomson, 'Population and depopulation', in D.J. Withrington ed., *Shetland and the Outside World 1469-1969*, Aberdeen 1983, pp.166-8; *Parliamentary Papers* 1884, xxxiii, minutes of evidence, pp.1409-10).
13. Sooth Cunningsburgh, Sumburgh estate. Scattald confiscated and sheep farm created c.1872 (*Parliamentary Papers* 1884, xxxiii, minutes of evidence, pp.1217-8, 1220-1, 1223, 1225-6, 1396-8; *Parliamentary Papers* 1895, xxxix, part 1, minutes of evidence, pp.1097-1104). 2,386 acres pasture scheduled by Deer Forest Commission.
14. Garth, Quendale estate, Dunrossness. Cleared 1874 and sheep farm created (Evershed, 'On the agriculture', p.213). 118 acres old arable and 495 pasture scheduled by Deer Forest Commission.

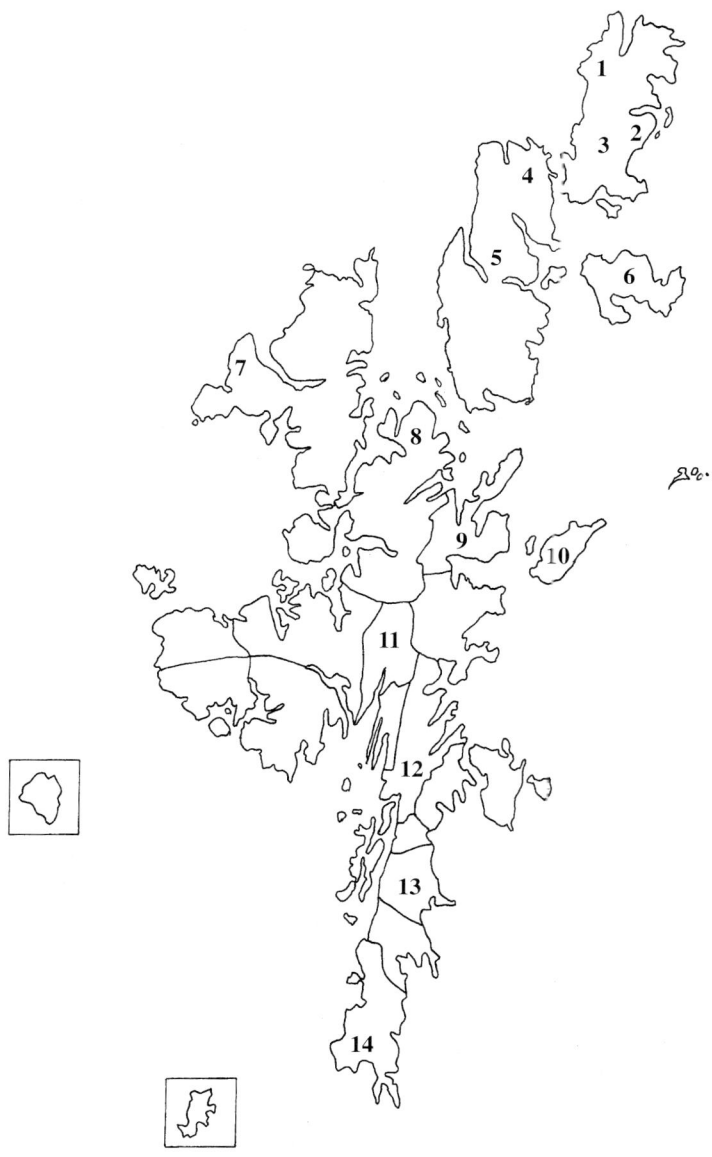

Figure 18 Major croft clearances and scattald confiscations in Shetland, c.1820-c.1875

scattalds on Major Cameron's Unst estates in the late 1860s. Spence & Co., who were heavily involved in fisheries in Unst, got a lease of the Garth estate there in 1867, and immediately sent a letter to all the tenants. They stated that there had been 'many vague reports throughout the island regarding the change of system in the management of the tenantry, consequent on the withdrawal from them of the scattalds'. Spence & Co. assured the tenants that 'the change was certain', but that they had decided to introduce it 'gradually and judiciously at first'.[224] Meanwhile, Alexander Sandison, one of the partners, was writing a vicious attack on John Walker, under the nom-de-plume 'Truckit Tammie', in which he posed as an Unst tenant under threat from a sheep farm.[225] This didn't prevent Sandison and his son from purchasing and leasing quite a few sheep-farms in Unst during the following decades: so many that the Tory *Shetland News* advised them, with deadly sarcasm, to hand them back to the crofters:[226]

> The whole thing may be done as an act of free good-will, and as a practical proof of the convicting influence of Liberal principles. If this hint is taken – as we have no doubt it will – it will be a fine example to set to some of those benighted Tories who continue to stick to their sheep farms and their grazing parks with all that tenacity for which they are so much abused.

The main result of these clearances was a decline in the population of specific areas, and a net fall in the total population of Shetland. As Walker himself confessed, rather ingenuously, 'unfortunately for the people themselves, about one half of our tenants in Delting and Yell left us).[227] The population of Shetland fell from 31,670 in 1861 to 29,705 in 1881. Much of this fall may be attributed to the disappearance of many of the emigrants' scattalds and crofts.

The Shetlanders who remained found that the sheep-farms had created a completely new kind of rural economy in some parishes. A remarkable editorial in the *Shetland Times* of 27 October 1888, describes what happened:

> At the time the sheep farming mania set in, a number of tenants had to remove, as their crofts were wanted, and the bulk of them settled down on other lands on the same estate, the landlord building their houses. If the crofter desired it, the house was roofed and fitted up for him. For this there was an increase of 7¼ per cent per annum on the rent of the croft; not, be it remembered, until the money so expended was repaid, but for all time coming. The best of the scattald was let to the sheep-farmers, and to prevent the crofters' animals straying on the pasture, it had to be fenced off, and to pay for this fence 7¼ per cent was added to the crofters' rents, and the crofters had to keep the original scattald fences in good repair. It was then found that the scattald was not sufficient for the number of animals, and to remove this grievance, the number of sheep was fixed at thirty head for every croft, a scattald tax of one shilling per head being charged for grazing. ... A few of the

---

224. *Parliamentary Papers* 1872, xxxv, appendix, pp.59-60.
225. *John o' Groat Journal*, 9 March 1871. I am pretty sure it is Sandison; it is difficult to imagine who else would have had the detailed knowledge and skill to write the piece.
226. *Shetland News*, 4 August 1894, editorial.
227. *Parliamentary Papers* 1871, xxxvi, minutes of evidence, p. 886.

Figures 19-20 Two photographs of the large 96-mark township of Gert in Dunrossness. In the first, taken by George Washington Wilson c.1870, Gert is a flourishing township with twenty families. In 1874 Andrew J. Grierson, the sole owner of Gert, evicted his tenants there. Around 1880 James Isbister photographed the desolate site. *Copyright Shetland Museum*

crofters had ponies, and for them a charge of 10s. a head was made, for grazing on the scattald. And more than that, for every pony put on the scattald, ten sheep had to be removed, as the pasture – if such it could be called – could not afford to keep the sheep and ponies also!

These allegations can be confirmed again and again from the evidence given to the Napier Commission of 1883, and to the fair rents tribunals of the Crofters Commission in 1889.[228] Hance Smith has written persuasively about the decline of the subsistence economy in late-nineteenth century Shetland, and the relocation of rural communities in prime fishing areas.[229] But he attributes these changes exclusively to alterations in the organization of the fisheries. Much of it was also due to the confiscation of the scattalds, and the rise in rents which ironically followed.

Reform and after

There is a strong impression among many Shetlanders today that the Crofters Holdings (Scotland) Act of 1886 put right these problems, and restored the scattalds to the Shetlanders without more ado. Certainly that was Lord Napier's intention. In his report he recommended that:

> the occupiers in an existing township should have the right to claim from the proprietor an enlargement of the existing township, in regard to arable land and common pasture.

If the proprietor didn't respond:

> the Sheriff Substitute should investigate the grounds of the claim, and if he finds it to be well-founded, he should record the township as an 'overcrowded township', and the claim as a reasonable claim. ... As leases expire, considerable areas of ground, especially of hill pasture, might be gradually recovered from farms and forests for the use of the crofting class.

And Napier singled out the Shetland scattalds for treatment in this way.[230]

But Napier's radical ideas didn't find their way into the Act.[231] One confrontation before the Crofters Commission in 1889 made that very clear.[232] In 1886 two tenants at Nissetter in Northmavine had heard a rumour that their landlord intended to enclose part of their scattald for the benefit of a crofter at the nearby township of Fiblister. They immediately wrote to him that 'our township has possessed [the scattald] in common with the township of Fiblister from time immemorial', and told him that 'the scat holds [sic] ... is to all intents and purposes part and parcel of our present holdings'. The landlord's agent replied that the estate had:

> no intention to deprive their tenants of the fair use of the scattalds, but at the same time the Trustees ... are bound ... to see that the property is made the most of, and

---

228. The Crofters Commission only printed the results of the fair rents enquiries. For almost verbatim accounts of the discussion – of absorbing interest to any historian of nineteenth-century Shetland – see the *Shetland Times* and *Shetland News*, August - November 1889.
229. Hance D. Smith, *Shetland Life and Trade 1550-1914*, Edinburgh 1984, pp.316f.
230. *Parliamentary Papers* 1884, xxxii, report, pp.24-6.
231. Clive Dewey, 'Celtic agrarian legislation and the Celtic Revival: historicist implications of Gladstone's Irish and Scottish Land Acts 1870-1886', *Past and Present*, 64, 1974, pp.63-8.
232. *Shetland Times,* 19 October 1889.

they must retain to themselves full power when they think it necessary and proper to enclose portions of the scattald.

The tenants took their case to the Crofters Commission, and the landlord's representative cross-examined them:

> 'You talk in the letter [he said], about a breach of your privileges. Now, what privileges had you at that date?'
> A.– 'We had the scattald.'
> Q.– 'But how long did the privileges last?'
> A.– 'As long as we remained tenants.'
> Q.– 'As long as the landlord chose to allow you to remain?'
> A.– 'Yes.'
> Q.– 'So that the landlord was not infringing any of your rights at this date?'
> A.– 'I don't see that.'
> Q.– 'You had no right to the scattald at that date except what the landlord gave you.'

The crofters' representative now intervened, to make the best of a bad job. 'I admit that,' he said. 'I knew he could have evicted them if he chose, but I say he did not give them any notice or warning.' Turning to the crofters he said: '"Did you get any notice or warning?" A.– "The notice consisted of wood and wire."'

Nonetheless the Shetlanders had high hopes of the Crofters Commission. Most people in the islands – crofters, intellectuals, the *Shetland Times* – were infected by the general glee. The intellectuals of late nineteenth century Shetland played an important part in the cultural life of the islands,[233] and almost all of them became identified with the crofters' cause – even the reactionaries. It is not surprising that Laurence Williamson, a crofter-scholar, felt moved to write a meticulously detailed account of the Fetlar clearances for the Commission,[234] or that the radical Haldane Burgess wrote a poem savaging 'Da fiends at drave da tenant furt'.[235] But Gilbert Goudie, a banker, wrote an article in the midst of the Crofters Commission hearings entitled 'Skathald', in which he stated that

> to enclose the Skathald as sheep runs, or otherwise deprive the people of free access and use of it, is not only an infringement of immemorial usage in the islands, but an outrage on the people's means and rights of existence.[236]

The *Shetland Times* immediately reprinted his piece, and applauded it in an editorial.[237] Arthur Laurenson, a hosiery merchant in Lerwick and scholar of Old Norse, had written an article attacking John Walker as early as 1872.[238] In 1894 he visited Unst, and wrote as follows to Catherine Spence:

> I went on ... to the old 'toon' of Cliff, all silent and deserted, no human habitation for miles, the bright green of the old arable land alone witnessing to what was for

---

233. Bronwen J. Cohen, 'Norse imagery in Shetland: an historical study of intellectuals and their use of the past in the construction of Shetland's identity, with particular reference to the period 1800-1914', unpublished university of Manchester Ph.D., 1983, pp.250-478.
234. Shetland Archives, D. 7/13/1.
235. J.J. Haldane Burgess, *Rasmie's Buddie*, Lerwick 1891, p.65.
236. *Scottish Leader*, 5 November 1889.
237. *Shetland Times*, 23 November and 7 December 1889.
238. Shetland Archives, D.3/11/1.

long centuries the dwellings of our race. The Scotch sheep-farmer has made Unst a desolation.[239]

Finally, the most startling radical of all: the authoress Jessie Saxby. She was a sister of David Charles Edmondston, who had carried out extensive clearances and scattald confiscations in Unst in the late 1860s, including those at Cliff. Jessie wrote that 'the people will never forgive the cruelty which robbed them of their "scattalds" ... which they passionately (and rightly) believed was theirs'.[240]

In a brilliant account of events in Sooth Cunningsburgh, where the confiscation of the scattald gave rise to fence-burning and what was called the 'Cunningsburgh Civil War', Marsha Renwanz has shown that the commissioners were sympathetic to the crofters as well.[241] The commissioners' first decisions, which gave fair rents to crofters throughout Shetland, and cancelled thousands of pounds worth of arrears, were very popular. But the scattalds were a far knottier problem, and after the commissioners had gone the *Shetland Times* remarked that it still 'remained to be grappled with'.[242] In fact the Government didn't face the problem squarely until the 1890s, and it wasn't until 1894 that the Deer Forest Commission, set up to find former crofting and pasture lands for new crofters' holdings, visited Shetland. By that time the public mood in Shetland had changed; radical crofters, especially those of Sooth Cunningsburgh, felt themselves far more isolated. The *Shetland Times* gave them no support, and deplored their attempts to take the law into their own hands. The commissioners were hostile. Renwanz calls this process 'the ideological fragmentation of the crofting community'.[243]

In due course the Deer Forest Commission scheduled 38,234 acres of pasture land and 2,614 acres of old arable for new crofters' holdings in Shetland and expansions of old ones.[244] But the Government did nothing to implement these recommendations. It wasn't until the 1920s[245] – in the case of Fetlar 1963! – that the Department of Agriculture resettled crofters on confiscated scattald land in a few areas.

By 1900 the ideological fragmentation of the crofting community, the physical fragmentation of it by sheep farms, and the impact of the new fisheries, had damaged the old rural communities in Shetland badly. Land settlement – if it came – was generally too meagre and too late to prevent depopulation. In 1900 an Unst landlord could still speak about 'the people's common scathold'[246], but he was a maverick. There are still large numbers of common grazings in Shetland.[247]

---

239. Catherine Spence, *Arthur Laurenson: his letters and literary remains*, London 1907, p.85.
240. Jessie M.E. Saxby, 'Shetland phrase and idiom, ii', *Old Lore Miscellany*, i, 1907-8, p.268.
241. Marsha Renwanz, 'From crofters to Shetlanders: the Social History of a Shetland Island Community's Self-Image 1872-1978', unpublished university of Stanford Ph.D., 1980, pp.82-5.
242. *Shetland Times*, 7 December 1889, editorial.
243. Renwanz, 'From crofters to Shetlanders', pp.93-9.
244. *Parliamentary Papers* 1895, xxxviii, appendix, pp.60-5.
245. Andrew C. O'Dell, *The Historical Geography of the Shetland Isles*, Lerwick 1939, pp.57-8; Leah Leneman, *Fit for Heroes? land settlement in Scotland after World War I*, Aberdeen 1989, pp.88-91, 220.
246. Shetland Archives, unlisted: Typed Muness estate instructions, signed by Thomas Dishington-Smith, 1900.
247. According to figures kindly supplied to me by Stewart Moore of the Department of Agriculture and Fisheries in 1984, there were then 96 common grazings in Shetland, extending to about 180,000 acres – although apportionments are always eating into this figure. For an account of crofters' common grazings in Scotland, which places the modern scattalds in the wider context of crofting law, see James R. Coull, 'Crofters' common grazings in Scotland', *Agricultural History Review*, xvi, 1968, pp.142-54.

Nowadays, however, they aren't neighbourhood units or the site of tenant-landlord struggles. What is a scattald in AD 2000? A shadow of its former self.

A note on waithing and waith

On 15 June 1603 the sheriff depute of Shetland held court at Gardie in Uyeasound, no doubt at the house of William Manson, Earl Patrick Stewart's bailie in Unst. Among other business he instructed Manson

> to mak compt, rakning and payment of the wathing of Burrafirthe, so far as concernis the kingis part of thrie merk land in Cliff, and of all yeiris bygaine sen the tyme of his office, reserving the action and question of that wathing to be discust be my lordis selff.[248]

'Wathing', or 'waithing', is a Scots word.[249] It means a catch of fish, the booty from a hunting expedition, or the act of fishing or hunting. Earl Patrick scrutinised every potential source of revenue in his dominions; hence his depute's instruction concerning the 'wathing' at Burrafirth, the northmost township on the west side of Unst.

Thirty-eight years later, on 21 April 1641, a woman called Gathrow Guttromesdoghter visited Gardie.[250] She was the widow of Tustian Turkelsone of 'Ilvesta', in the parish of 'Buckney' in Norway – almost certainly the modern Alvestad in Bokn in Stavanger.[251] Her parents Guttrome Petersone and Margaret

Figure 21 The waithing skerries of Burrafirth, photographed by Jack Rattar in the 1930s. *Copyright Shetland Museum*

---

248. Gordon Donaldson ed., *The Court Book of Shetland 1602-1604*, Edinburgh 1954, p.69.
249. *Oxford English Dictionary* ('Waithing').
250. National Archives of Scotland, RS.44/3, folio 219 verso.
251. O. Rygh ed., *Norske Gaardnavne*, x, Kristiania 1915, p.432. I am grateful to Alfhild Nakken, Riksarkivet, Oslo, for advice concerning this place.

Halstensdoghter, and her maternal grandfather Halsten Olasone, had been 'righteous udallers and roithismen' of estates in Shetland. Gathrow now disposed of these estates, in Unst, Yell and Whalsay, to Magnus Henderson of Gardie, William Manson's grandson. Among the lands she sold were eight marks of land in Westhous in Burrafirth, 'with the waithing skerrie proper thairof callit the West Holme or Skerrie of Burrafirth'.

Waithing skerries

Gathrow's transaction helps us to understand the 'wathing of Burrafirth'. The 'West Holme or Skerrie' is without doubt the islet which appears on the Ordnance Survey map as Vesta Skerry, one of the southmost of the holms which lie north of Hermaness. Another of the holms is called Cliff Skerry, named after the township of Cliff, immediately south of Burrafirth; a third is Tipta Skerry, which may have taken its name from the house called Toft (Old Norse *topt*) in Burrafirth, or from the adjacent township of Tupton. It is clear that the settlements in the north-west corner of Unst had more or less exclusive rights to seals and birds, and other 'waithing', on these well-favoured holms. 'Upon the west side of the bay [of Burrafirth]', says an anonymous writer around 1680,[252]

> there ly several rocks or skerries, which selcks frequent in the month of November, and the inhabitants neglect not to wait upon them to kill them. The skins they sell, but the bouks they salt; and in time of Lent they eat them as sweetly as venison.

We don't find many references to 'waithing' in Shetland documents. As time went on Shetlanders spent more and more time in commercial rather than subsistence fishing. Prosperous landowners snapped up more and more land, and as a result privileges pertaining to individual townships and scattalds were whittled away. As we have seen, it was the proprietor of part of Burrafirth who owned the 'waithing skerrie' at Burrafirth in 1641, and the reference to the 'wathing of Burrafirthe' in 1603 suggests that an individual, William Manson, had been meddling with it. (Note that on that occasion Earl Patrick Stewart was trying to maintain the rights of the township of Cliff to the waithing of Burrafirth – because he owned three marks of land there.) And in 1593 Earl Patrick feued to his servant Thomas Knychtsone various lands in Bressay, with the 'fischingis, waithing, halking [and] hunting' there.[253]

Wreck and waith

Elsewhere in the 1593 document Earl Patrick reserves for his own use 'the wrack and waith that sall fortoun [i.e. chance] to cum in the said ile'. Here we encounter 'waith' for the first time. Patrick seems to be making a distinction between 'waithing', the right to fisheries around Bressay, and 'wreck and waith', by which he meant flotsam and jetsam on the shore. However, Scots 'waith' originally meant much the same as Old Norse *veiðr*, which in turn meant the same as waithing. In

---

252. J. Bruce ed., *Description of ye Countrey of Zetland*, Edinburgh 1908, p.76.
253. Shetland Archives, GD.144/24/4.

Blind Harry's poem about William Wallace, written in the 1470s, some Englishmen demand fish from Wallace and his son. Wallace says obligingly:[254]
    '...me think yhe suld half part.
    Waith suld be delt in all place with fre hart.'
    He bade his child, 'Gyff thaim of our waithyng.'
And in a Shetland document of 1431, concerning rights pertaining to the townships of Garth, Crookster and Caldback in Delting, several local arbiters stated that 'skall Gerdis oc Kruxsatris bera up vade oc raka effthir skatte semom y Kaldbaxnis' (Garth and Crookster shall bear up 'vade' and 'rak' in proportion to their scat in Caldbackness). A Scots notary who copied the document c.1550 translated that sentence: 'sell Geartht and Cruxsatre tak owp dryffin tymmyr and [fische *deleted*] waiding efther thair skat in Kaldbaxnes'. In other words, 'vade' = 'fische' = 'waiding'.[255]

'Waith' appears more often in Shetland and Orkney documents than 'waithing', usually, as in the 1431 and 1593 cases, in conjunction with the word 'wreck'. When Adam Bothwell feued his bishopric lands in Shetland to Robert Stewart, in 1572, he included 'wrak, waith [and] half wrak',[256] and five years later Andrew Mowat of Hogaland disponed the 'wraik [and] waithe' of lands in Delting and elsewhere to his sons.[257] In 1615 the sheriff court of Shetland ordered that 'na persone ... sall hyde ... ony kynd of thift, sorcerie ... wrak or ony kynd of waith'.[258] There can be no doubt that Shetlanders had pursued waith, or *veiðr*, for centuries. At first sight it is surprising that there are not more references to their activity in documents. We should keep in mind, however, that its heyday was no doubt in medieval times, and we have very few Shetland documents from that era. There is no reason to think that *veiðr* in Shetland was less important than in, say, Iceland, where it is well-attested.[259] One way to find traces of it in Shetland is to look at place-names. Da Vadament Stack at Woodwick in Unst, rendered Da Vedemanstakk by Jakobsen, is without doubt from Old Norse *veiðimann*, fisherman.[260] Similarly, Da Veeda Stack at Huxter in Whalsay derives from *veiðr*. Jakobsen recorded another such name, Da Vjedemanso, now apparently lost, at the Westing of Unst. All these places are rocks where Shetlanders fished at the shore: so-called 'craeg-saets'.[261]

A far more important spot for waith in Shetland was the Vee Skerries, rocks north-west of the island of Papa Stour. Jakobsen derived the name from Old Norse *vaða*, to wade, but Vee Skerries is without doubt another *veiðr*-name.[262] A document of 1609 refers to Andrew Mowat's valuable 'fischingis in Veaskerie',[263] and there are

---

254. Matthew P. McDiarmid ed., *Hary's Wallace*, i, Edinburgh 1968, p.14.
255. John H. Ballantyne and Brian Smith eds., *Shetland Documents 1195-1579*, Lerwick 1999, no. 21.
256. John H. Ballantyne and Brian Smith eds., *Shetland Documents 1195-1579*, Lerwick 1999, no. 193. Presumably 'half' is a mistake for 'haff', ocean.
257. John H. Ballantyne and Brian Smith eds., *Shetland Documents 1195-1579*, Lerwick 1999, no. 235.
258. Gordon Donaldson ed., *The Court Book of Shetland 1615-1629*, Lerwick 1991, p.164.259. Kirstin Hastrup, *Nature and Policy in Iceland 1400-1800*, Oxford 1990, pp.68-9, 74.
259. Kirstin Hastrup, *Nature and Policy in Iceland 1400-1800*, Oxford 1990, pp. 68-9, 74.
260. Jakob Jakobsen, *Place-names of Shetland*, London 1936, p.137.
261. There are of course *veiðr*-names outwith Shetland. An important example is the Brig of Waith in Orkney, presumably so-called because of fish netted there: J. Storer Clouston, 'Something about Maeshowe', *Proceedings of the Orkney Antiquarian Society*, xi, 1932-3, p.15.
262. Cf. Vesker in Birsay in Orkney, 'a notable rock fishing site', which Hugh Marwick derives from *veiði-sker*: Hugh Marwick, *The Place-names of Birsay*, Aberdeen 1970, p.3.
263. John H. Ballantyne and Brian Smith eds., *Shetland Documents 1580-1611*, Lerwick 1994, no. 482.

vivid traditional tales of sealing expeditions there.[264] In 1723 James Mouat leased to Arthur Nicolson 72 marks of land in Papa Stour,[265] with

> a proportional part of all whaills [and] selchy waithing in Veaskerrys, and wrackts and other casuall and accidentall things that may be drove ashoar on ... Papa, and salved by the inhabitants thereof, effeiring and corresponding to his seventy two merk land.

A little-known eighteenth century account describes the produce of the Vee Skerries as follows:[266]

> These rocks, which in boisterous weather wear a dreadful appearance from the horn of Papa Stour, have yet been known to shelter men and boats, when defeated or overtaken by a high sea, on their returning from the ling fishing. ... Besides this convenience, they shelve so much, that boats can be drawn up and secured upon them. Nay, there is an instance of a lodge having been erected there by Dunrossness men, for a fishing station. They have not a sward of grass, but abound in limpets of a large size. They also produce flint; and are much resorted to by seals. In fine, these Skerries may be considered as an appendage of Papa, although considerably disjoined from it. At all events, they are a great convenience.

Seal-waith

The Vee Skerries were thus 'waithing skerries', exactly like the Skerries of Burrafirth. They belonged to the proprietors and inhabitants of Papa Stour, just as Vesta Skerry was a 'convenience' to the people of Burrafirth. Andrew Mowat (see above) leased Papa from its owners in Norway, and he simultaneously leased its *veiðr*. There is evidence from a document of 1490 that Shetland lands, not least Papa, were especially coveted for the seals which sojourned on their adjacent islets. In that year arbiters split the great estates of Hans Sigurdsson, a Norwegian nobleman, into three portions. They divided his Shetland lands into three properties as well, based on Papa Stour, Vaila and Noss. There are references in the document to Papa 'med sith sielwede' (with its seal-waith); Vaila 'med thy selweide ther vnder ligger' (with the seal-waith which lies under it); and Noss 'med sielewede som dher till hører' (with the seal-waith that belongs to it).[267]

Another great seal-skerry was – and is – the Muckle Skerry, north-west of the Out Skerries.[268] This must be the islet referred to as Selchiskerry in older documents.[269] In 1634 the minister of Nesting pursued the laird of Brough in the Court of Session, for teinds of seals 'slain yeirlie in waithing in Selchiskerrie' in the 1620s and early 1630s.[270] Forty years later Hugh Sinclair of Brough sold his islands around the Out Skerries to David Murray of Clairden. Among them were 'the Meikle and Litle Skerries ... with the waithing and killing of shelkies furth of aither of them'.[271]

---

264. Calum MacLean recorded Brucie Henderson on the subject in 1955: School of Scottish Studies, tape 1955/93.
265. Shetland Archives, GD.144/168/19.
266. 'C.S.', 'Descriptive sketch of the island Papa Stour, Shetland', *Bee,* xiii, 1793, p.302.
267. John H. Ballantyne and Brian Smith eds., *Shetland Documents 1195-1579,* Lerwick 1999, no. 32.
268. See the map in R.J. Berry and J.L. Johnson, *The Natural History of Shetland,* London 1980, p.115.
269. Selchiskerrie was valuable enough to be measured in marks of land: John H. Ballantyne and Brian Smith eds., *Shetland Documents 1580-1611,* Lerwick 1994, no. 99.
270. National Archives of Scotland, CS.7/468, folios 179-81.
271. National Archives of Scotland, RS.45/3, folio 352. I am grateful to John Ballantyne for reminding me about this document.

It is likely that seals were the most important denizens of waithing skerries and holms. Shetlanders visited such holms with seal-nets,[272] and, as time went on, proprietors took steps to keep them out. In July 1603 Earl Patrick's court made an ordinance 'that nane frequent ony of my lordis holmis with ony selchie nets without leife'.[273]

The Atlantic Ocean and the North Sea are full of seals, and the arrangements we find in Shetland have parallels elsewhere. Adomnán, in his seventh century life of Columba, refers to what sounds very like a waithing skerry belonging to Iona.[274] Columba preserved the seals there from a robber. Norwegians were also jealous concerning their seals. Magnus Lagabøter's Landlaw – the great law-code used throughout Norway and in Shetland from the thirteenth to the seventeenth centuries – contains a special section 'um sela ueiðar': on seal-waith.[275] Documents about lands in sixteenth century Norway frequently refer to their associated seal-skerries and seal-holms.[276]

Waith and waifs

In conclusion, I return for a moment to the word 'waith' and its etymology. There can be little doubt, from the evidence assembled above, that 'waith' in Shetland derives from Old Norse *veiðr*, and means the same as (and may sometimes be affected by) Scots 'waith'. Scholars and lexicographers, on the other hand, suggest that our waith is an 'altered form' of the English word 'waif', meaning a poor lost soul, or 'something loose or wandering'.[277] I imagine that their error derives from a notion that, in the phrase 'wreck and waith', waith simply means wreck-wood – something that 'wanders' round the shore.[278] As we have seen, it meant something far more complex.

It is easy to see why the lexicographers came to their conclusion. I suspect that, at a very early date, Scots writers began to confuse waith and waif. An intermediate stage in the confusion seems to appear in a Shetland document of 1590, where Earl Patrick Stewart instructs his bailie in Yell to claim for him all 'wrak, waith and waiff guddis'.[279] Around 1510 Gavin Douglas, translating the *Aeneid*, said that [280]

> ... Virgil sawis ar worth to put in stor.
> Thay aucht not to be hald vagabund nor waith–
> Ful riche tresour thai bene and precius graith ...

---

272. For a good account of the use of seal-nets in Shetland, albeit at a much later date, see Arthur Edmondston, *A View of the Ancient and Present State of the Zetland Islands*, ii, Edinburgh 1809, pp.292-3, 295.
273. Gordon Donaldson ed., *The Court Book of Shetland 1602-1604*, Edinburgh 1954, p.83.
274. A.O. Anderson and M.O. Anderson eds., *Adomnan's Life of Columba*, London etc. 1961, p.294.
275. Magnus Lagabøter's Landlaw VII.65, in R. Keyser and P.A. Munch eds, *Norges Gamle Love indtil 1387*, ii, Christiania 1845, p.145.
276. Odd Vollan, 'Säljakt', in *Kulturhistorisk Leksikon for Nordisk Middelalder*, xvii, Copenhagen 1981, cols. 695-9.277.
277. An early example is J. Ritson ed., *Robin Hood, a collection of all ancient poems, songs and ballads*, London 1795, p. 1xxv. See also *Oxford English Dictionary* ('Waith', sb.2 and 'Waif', sb.1), and *Scottish National Dictionary* ('Waith', n.1.)
278. I suspect too that 'wreck' originally had a far wider meaning than mere sea-driven wood. The Icelandic law-code Grágás includes in *reki* 'timber and whale and seal, fish and bird and seaweed' (cited in G. Vigusson, *An Icelandic-English Dictionary*, Oxford 1975 ['*reki*']). In other words, *reki* meant much the same as *veiðr*, except that *veiðr* meant things that were hunted, *reki* things stranded.
279. John H. Ballantyne and Brian Smith eds., *Shetland Documents 1580-1611*, Lerwick 1994, no. 174.
280. D.F.C. Coldwell ed., *Virgil's 'Aeneid' translated into Scottish verse by Gavin Douglas*, iii, Edinburgh and London 1959, p.3.

'Waith' in this case can scarcely mean the same as *veiðr!* Douglas almost certainly had in mind 'waif'.

Furthermore, there are real similarities between the vocabulary of waithing and that of waifs. Waif-references sometimes involve property-rights, and seashores, or both. In Scott's *Woodstock* (1826) Sir Henry Lee announces that he is keeper of Woodstock Park, 'with right of waif and stray, vert and venison'.[281] Charles Kingsley, in *Hereward the Wake* (1866),[282] describes country people 'prowling about the shore after the waifs of the storm, deserted jetsom and lagend'. Bulwer Lytton even managed to create a verb out of waif: In *Harold, the last of the Saxon kings* (1848) the count of Ponthieu is said to have 'right of life and death over all stranded and waifed on his coast'.[283]

*

To sum up. *Veiðr*, hunting, was a common but not well-documented activity in medieval and early modern Shetland. In some cases it was a privilege attached to landed property. 'Waith' meant the same as Scots 'waithing'. Scots also had a word 'waith', with the same meaning. But at an early date Scots writers began to confuse their 'waith' with English 'waif', and in due course the lexicographers followed them. Eventually Scots 'waith' came to mean nothing but sea-driven wood and stranded whales.

Figure 22 The results of a 'caa' (hunt) of 70 or so bottlenose whales, on the beach at Sand, Sandsting, in July 1899 (photographer Tom Kent). The captors have cut off and divided the 'spik' (blubber), which will be rendered down for oil. The 'crangs' are left on the beach to rot. *Copyright Shetland Museum*

---

281. Chapter 2.
282. Chapter 6.
283. Book 9, chapter 1.

4
Rents from the sea

Adam Smith wrote a paragraph about Shetland in the first book of *The Wealth of Nations*.[284] It was elegant, accurate, and theoretically acute:

> The sea in the neighbourhood of the islands of Shetland is more than commonly abundant in fish, which makes a great part of the subsistence of their inhabitants. But in order to profit by the produce of the water, they must have habitation upon the neighbouring land. The rent of the landlord is in proportion, not to what the farmer can make by the land, but to what he can make both by the land and the water. It is partly paid in sea-fish; and one of the very few instances in which rent makes a part of the price of that commodity is to be found in that country.

It is difficult to know where Smith gleaned this information. I suspect he got it from a Shetlander, or a visitor to Shetland, because in the 1770s there was as yet no good published account of Shetland's political economy

Fishing tenure

Smith's brief remark was the beginning of critical writing about Shetland. He presents Shetland's tenurial system as a curiosity. Did it resemble anything elsewhere in the world? A.J. Youngson has suggested that the organisation of the Shetland fishing industry in Smith's time involved

> a system very much like share-cropping in the American South, fifty to a hundred years later, where shortage of credit made necessary the pledging of cotton crops to merchants against seed and future supplies.[285]

Share-cropping is easy to describe: 'an owner of cultivated land agrees to make it available to a supplier of labour in return for a fixed proportion of the output'.[286] This is half-way to a description of Shetland's political economy in the 1770s. However, there were special features of the Shetland variant of peasant bondage which have made it difficult to categorise, and have made Shetland historians chary about fitting it into a general framework.[287] As Adam Smith said, Shetland provided 'one of the very few instances' where the crop involved in a tenancy contract was fish. Shetlanders didn't give their landlords a fixed proportion of *one* crop (the norm in share-cropping); they gave them the *whole* proceeds of their summer fishing. In

---
284. Adam Smith, *The Wealth of Nations*, Book I, chapter 11.
285. A.J. Youngson, *After the Forty-Five: the economic impact on the Scottish Highlands*, Edinburgh 1973, p.108.
286. W.G. Runciman, *A Treatise on Social Theory, ii: substantive social theory*, Cambridge 1989, p.304.
287. Even Richard Smith, 'Shetland in the world economy: a sociological history of the 18th and 19th centuries', unpublished university of Edinburgh Ph.D., 1986, despite his title, portrays Shetland fishing tenure as a closed, local, 'system', without comparing it with anything elsewhere.

Figure 23 The 'sixern' (six-oared boat) *Break of Day* – by now a flitboat – is being rowed ashore at Symbister, c.1904 (photographer Tom Kent). Ashore is Messrs Hay & Co.'s white-fish station. Men are splitting fish; afterwards the fish will be carted to dry on the beach (left), where 'steeples' of fish under tarpaulins are lying already. George Couper's herring station is on the right. *Copyright Shetland Museum.*

addition they paid a (low) land-rent, in butter and cash. On some estates the tenants were 'bound' to hand over some of their farm produce as well: butter, oil, animals, and so on. In return they received land, whose rent was extinguished, or not extinguished in bad years, by fish, in accordance with fixed prices assigned by the landlords themselves.

In other words, Shetland's system was more complex than those where tenants gave up this or that proportion of their crop: a third, a half, or more; and as a result the Shetland mode didn't have a name like the French 'metayage', which denotes 'half' the crop, or the Ghanaian 'abusa', which means 'one-third'.[288] The first comprehensive term assigned to peasant bondage in Shetland, a rather fine one, which I shall use throughout this chapter, was 'fishing tenure', coined by Samuel Hibbert about 1820.[289]

Fishing tenure in Shetland may appear to have been a convenient relationship between landowner and tenant, with equal benefits for both sides – and without coercion on the part of the landlord. Such arrangements usually make their appearance in societies where land is scarce. As Smith said, 'in order to profit by the produce of the water, [the Shetlanders] must have a habitation upon the neighbouring land'. The key point about fishing tenure is that the Shetland landowners evicted their tenants from these habitations, or led them to believe that they would evict them, if they didn't fish for them. 'We knew quite well', said James

---

288. A.F. Robertson, 'On share-cropping', *Man*, new series, xv, 1980, p.416.
289. Samuel Hibbert, *A Description of the Shetland Islands,* Edinburgh 1822, p.515. The notion that Shetland fishing tenure was called 'the Shetland Method', entertained by some historians, is incorrect.

Flaws, a tenant on the Quendale estate in 1872, 'from the statement which was made to us before, that if anyone transgressed the rule, the penalty would just be our forty days' warning'.[290]

Finally, the question of debt and debt-bondage arises again and again, not as an integral feature of fishing tenure, but as a feature which often accompanied it, especially following years of famine. When landlords gave credit, when they gave the Shetlanders goods from their truck-shops, chronic indebtedness for the tenants inevitably followed.

I hope that these introductory remarks outline the main characteristics of fishing tenure in Shetland. They have certainly done nothing to pinpoint the main problems. I now proceed to tackle those in an orderly way.

First, we have to look at the *preconditions* for fishing tenure, and secondly at its *chronology*. If we ignore these questions of the origin and what we might call the speed and rhythm of fishing tenure, we may conclude that it was age-old and 'natural' – or that it was more short-lived than in fact it was.

It is essential, in the third place, to look in close detail at the tenancy contracts themselves, and the attitudes of the landowners and tenants to their rights and obligations. How uneasy were the landlords? and how alienated were the tenants?

Finally, we have to explore the vexed question of how change finally came in Shetland society, not much more than a century ago. In some ways this is the most puzzling question of all. If we can formulate all the questions clearly, about the preconditions, the chronology, the psychology and the disappearance of fishing tenure in Shetland, we may begin to understand it.

Preconditions

There were three preconditions for fishing tenure in Shetland: the first two long-term and the last temporary and climactic. The first was Shetland's medieval tenurial relationships; the second was her early and long-lived experience of trade and commerce; the third was the crisis which afflicted the islands in the seventeenth century.

Adam Smith, and a whole series of neo-classicists and Marxists who came after him, argued that share-cropping was a half-way house between slavery and agrarian capitalism. If that is a rule Shetland is not a good example of it. Slavery disappeared from Shetland, as from Norway as a whole, in the high middle ages, and was gradually replaced by tenancy arrangements which were 'free'. In the late thirteenth century royal administrators in Shetland formulated a local variant of the tenancy structure laid down for use throughout the kingdom in King Magnus Lagabøter's Landlaw. Like Norway, Shetland during the middle ages was a 'land of tenants', and the Shetlanders' lands were divided up, and taxed, according to the amount of land-rent the king's servants had decided they were able to pay.[291]

I said a moment ago that the Shetland tenants were relatively free. There is very little sign of manorial farms in the islands; Shetlanders usually lived in small peasant townships, fragments of which were owned by greater or lesser landlords, some of whom lived locally, and some of whom lived in Norway. By the sixteenth

---

290. *Parliamentary Papers* 1872, xxxv, minutes of evidence, p.122.
291. See Chapter 1, *supra*.

century, when we first have detailed rentals, there was very little crown or bishopric land in the islands, leaving royal and ecclesiastical officials to concentrate on legal matters, which they did in conjunction with local tribunes of the people.[292]

Historians have often painted a melodramatic picture of landholding relationships in Shetland following the events of 1469, when the king of Denmark mortgaged his rights in the islands to the king of Scotland. The historians portray a scenario where greedy Scotsmen confiscated land from peasant proprietors and transformed the peasants into serfs. No doubt there were larger numbers of small landowners in Shetland in the middle ages than there were later, but there had always been plenty of tenants, and their status didn't alter. In any case, peasant proprietors have their own problems: problems arising from subdivision of land among heirs, and the likelihood that, in bad times, land may become security for debt. 'A tenant might well suffer less than a freeholder, especially perhaps if the tenant was a share-cropper'.[293]

Perhaps it is too bold to say that share-croppers are better off than tenants, except in very special circumstances. Tenancy relationships in medieval Norway were relatively favourable to the tenants. The Shetlanders paid land-rent according to formulae laid down in the thirteenth century, which were adhered to and enforced, with relatively minor modification, during the subsequent centuries (see Chapter 1, *supra*). They didn't pay rents in fish: they *ate* and *sold* fish. There is no evidence at all that landowners found it feasible to alter these rents – except downwards, when they found it impossible to find tenants.

In the seventeenth century, then, Shetlanders were tenants, but not yet enmeshed in peasant bondage. In many ways their relative freedom was reinforced by their relationships with the outside world. Historians have often described the sudden arrival in Shetland in the fifteenth century of merchants from North Germany as the moment when the islanders first experienced the world of trade and markets.[294] But Shetlanders had been exposed to commerce at an even earlier period. In the high middle ages trade between Norway and the 'scatlands', colonies like Shetland in the west, was in the hands of small merchants organised in brotherhoods, exactly as the Germans organised themselves in later centuries. In the late thirteenth century, when Shetland's landholding structures were being enshrined in law, the kings of Norway were trying to regulate this trade as a monopoly, just as the Hansa tried to keep their Shetland-faring merchants in order later in the fifteenth and sixteenth centuries.[295]

The Shetlanders, then, knew about the word of commerce from a very early date. When I say that their tenurial freedom was reinforced by their relationships with the outside world, I don't just mean that individual Shetlanders bargained with the Germans about their own fish, although that was the case. I was referring to the extremely healthy state of local government in the islands in the period up to the early seventeenth century. Local officials in Shetland regulated the activities, the locations and even the prices charged by foreign merchants in the islands, once again

---

292. Brian Smith, 'Shetland, Scotland and Scandinavia, 1400-1700: the changing nature of contact', in G. Simpson ed., *Scotland and Scandinavia*, Edinburgh 1990, p.30.
293. Geoffrey de Ste. Croix, *The Class Struggle in the Ancient Greek World*, London 1981, p.214.
294. Hance D. Smith, *Shetland Life and Trade*, Edinburgh 1984, p.289.
295. Grethe Authén Blom, 'Skattland', in *Kulturhistorisk Leksikon for Nordisk Middelalder*, xv, Copenhagen 1981, cols. 446-50.

in accordance with laws promulgated around 1300.[296] Summing up: Shetlanders in 1600, the great-grandparents of the debt-bound peasants of later times, weren't serfs: they were free in a tenurial sense, and positively forceful in their relationships with the outside world of commerce. Their freedom was long-established, and when there were attempts to encroach on it they complained bitterly.[297]

The change came in the seventeenth century, which in Shetland was one long crisis. In the first decades of the century the local government structures collapsed, and the administration of law fell into the hands of local landowners. Famines and fevers afflicted the islands from the 1620s onwards, and came to a head in the 1690s,

Figure 24 The 'bød' (booth) and beach at Hillswick, Northmavine, photographed by John Irvine c.1880. Large numbers of fish are drying on the beach. At the head of the beach are boats in their 'nousts': three 'sixerns' in front and a 'fourern' behind. The weighing apparatus is in the middle of the beach; around it tarpaulins are spread to dry. Boys watch the fish: when rain comes they must rush to stack them up and cover them with tarpaulins. *Copyright Shetland Museum*

impoverishing tenants and landowners simultaneously. Few landlords had interests other than the rents of their fragmentary estates, the strictly regulated rents I've already described. In the years at the turn of the century several of them went bankrupt. The population of the islands was at a low ebb, especially after a particularly severe attack of smallpox in 1700.[298] Worst of all, from the point of view

---

296. Brian Smith, 'Shetland, Scandinavia, Scotland, 1300-1700: the changing nature of contact', in Grant Simpson ed., *Scotland and Scandinavia* 800-1800, Edinburgh 1990, p.31.
297. Rereading this passage, ten years after first writing it, I see that it is a rosy account. The German merchants had no control over the Shetlanders' tenancy arrangements; but they had a crucial and not-much-studied effect on the islands' economic self-sufficiency. They made themselves indispensable to the Shetlanders by paying in advance for goods yet to be delivered. The result was that the Shetlanders failed to create their own commercial economy, or even a town. For situations of this kind see Marian Malowist 'A certain trade technique in the Baltic countries in the 15th-17th centuries', in *Poland at the XIth International Congress of Historical Sciences*, Warsaw 1960, pp.103ff.
298. Brian Smith, 'Camphor, cabbage leaves and vaccination: the career of Johnie "Notions" Williamson of Hamnavoe, Eshaness, Shetland', *Proceedings of the Royal College of Physicians of Edinburgh*, xxviii 1998, pp.395ff.

of the tenants and their feckless landlords, the German merchants stopped coming to Shetland, because of the hopeless economic and international situation, and, the last straw, difficulties placed in their way by the Act of Union.[299]

This was the scenario in the islands when several local merchants, in a matter of a few years, bought up and leased bankrupt estates in Shetland, took over the fishing trade as Shetland's first local merchant class, and devised fishing tenure as a means of binding their new tenants and subtenants. It is to the era of the merchant-lairds, the era of fishing tenure, that I now turn.

'Whoever coms here to buy fish most have them of the landmaster'

Relationships such as share-cropping are extremely difficult to pin down in the historical record. As one social anthropologist has written:[300]

> the actual process of negotiation has rarely been observed and described, perhaps because it may be so tacit, so subtle or so protracted as to defy the patience of the most devoted fieldworker.

There is no knowing precisely when the Shetland merchant-landlords first entered into agreements with their tenants about the latter's fish. We do, however, have documents where the arrangement is referred to obliquely. Not surprisingly, the first of them dates from the 1690s, and had its origin in the crisis of that decade.[301] In 1695 Laurence Sinclair of Quendale, a landlord in the South Mainland of Shetland, found himself confronted with a bill for 5,600 merks Scots for superior duties to the crown, which he was unable to pay. He sought out four Dundee merchants who had been frequenting the district for some time, and came to an agreement with them. They gave him the money, and he promised them[302]

> in a trew ... fourth pairt devisione, the haill fisching and oylie that shall be taken and woon by my tennents and servants in the Fairyle and be my tennents in the ... parochen of Dunrossnes.

The merchants and Sinclair bound themselves to pay 1,000 merks Scots if either of them broke the contract. It is crystal clear, especially from this penalty clause, that both Sinclair and his creditors were confident that Sinclair's tenants would deliver the goods.

It is not until the first decade of the eighteenth century, however, that we discover local parties in the role of merchants themselves. Interestingly enough, the estate and tenants involved in the first such case known to me are the same as those in the 1695 contract I've just mentioned. The Sinclairs of Quendale were still in

---

299. Brian Smith, '"Lairds" and "improvement" in Shetland in the seventeenth and eighteenth centuries', in T.M. Devine ed., *Lairds and Improvement in the Scotland of the Enlightenment*, Glasgow 1979, p.13.
300. A.F. Robertson, 'On share-cropping', *Man*, new series, xv, 1980, p.418.
301. John Ballantyne has now drawn my attention to a contract of 1657 between the Shetland proprietor Laurence Sinclair of Brough, and James Broun, a Fife skipper, where Sinclair gives Broun 'licence and tollerance ... to goe with his bark and boat to my port and heavine of Skerries', for four years, 'and thair to buy all kind of fishes quhatsoevir frome the fishermen, takeris thairof' (National Archives of Scotland, CS.15, box 306). Sinclair also undertakes that during this period he 'sall not suffer ... any persone ... of whatsoevir nationes to goe or rowe in to the said port and harbure of Skerries to buy any fishes whatsoevir ... bot the said James Broun.' This may imply that there was fishing tenure on Sinclair's estate, at a very early date. It makes me wonder if Shetland landowners might have made similar bargains with German merchants that we know nothing about.
302. Shetland Archives, SC.12/53/1, pp.46-8: Registered contract between Laurence Sinclair and others.

severe financial difficulties – in fact they never escaped from them – and on this occasion they had leased their estate to Thomas Gifford, the foremost of the merchant-lairds who had emerged in Shetland during the crisis years. In April 1707 Gifford entered into a contract with three other merchant-lairds – James Mitchell of Girlsta, William Henderson of Gardie and Arthur Nicolson of Bullister – in which he obliged himself to make the Quendale tenants fish for those merchants and no-one else.[303]

In this case we have fishing tenure in its final form. It isn't a necessary condition of share-cropping that the tenant must hand her crop to a landlord rather than a lessee. As we shall see, lessees continued to be an important component of Shetland fishing tenure until the late nineteenth century. However, people like Thomas Gifford were not slow in building up their own estates, often by buying up ready-made estates from bankrupt neighbours.

It is difficult to be certain about how quickly fishing tenure became general in Shetland. My guess is that by 1720 most landlords had introduced it, either directly, by engaging in trade themselves, or by leasing their estates to one of the local merchants. In 1718 Thomas Gifford informed a merchant in Edinburgh[304] who had expressed an interest in coming to Shetland to buy fish

> that now of late all the people in Zettland that have land doth seperalie take and cure all the fishes caught by their own tenants, and doth ather export them themselves or sells them in the cuntrie, so that now whoever coms here to buy fish most have them of the landmaster but not of the fisher men.

One could argue that, even with a scenario like this, fishing was not actually a condition of tenure. But on Gifford's own estate it definitely was: in 1726 he wrote that his 'oun tenants ... stand bound by ther tacks under a failie' if they refused to fish for him.[305] It is difficult to believe that his colleagues would have had different arrangements.

I want to stress the point that, right from the beginning of fishing tenure in Shetland to the end, a century and a half later, we find merchant-lairds who deal with other merchants and lease their estates to them. In each case the tenants were bound by unwritten or (rarely) written leases to deliver their fish to a merchant or merchant-landlord.[306] I labour this point because some Shetland historians have argued that there was a qualitative difference between class relations in eighteenth century Shetland and those of the nineteenth century, where fish-exporting landlords were replaced by fish-exporting merchants. According to this interpretation the landlords bound their tenants with fishing tenure and later the merchants enmeshed them in debt. The historians who argue in this way are Smithians – not least the doyen of them, my friend Hance Smith, whose book *Shetland Life and Trade* is articulated around that thesis. For historians like Hance Smith the Shetland bourgeoisie of the nineteenth century, the 'Shetland Traders', as he calls them, were a more efficient replacement for their landlord predecessors.[307]

---

303. Shetland Archives, GD. 144/259/9: Contract between Thomas Gifford and others.
304. R. Stuart Bruce, 'The haaf fishing and Shetland trading', *Mariner's Mirror*, viii, 1922, p.51.
305. See Appendix, p.90, *infra*.
306. For four examples of written contracts see Appendix, pp.94-7, *infra*.
307. Hance D. Smith, *Shetland Life and Trade 1550-1914*, Edinburgh 1984, pp.93ff.

I argue for the 'persistence of the old regime'. There is little or no difference, in essentials, between a merchant-laird like Thomas Gifford, who presided over fishing tenure in its original form, and John Bruce of Sumburgh and Andrew Grierson of Quendale, two merchant-lairds who forced their Dunrossness tenants to fish for them in the 1870s. (Apart, that is, from the fact that Bruce and Grierson allowed their tenants market prices rather than fixed ones.) There were, indeed, estates in the 1870s which were run by merchant houses, and I shall deal with one of them in more detail later, but in the early eighteenth century, as we have seen, merchants leased estates.

It would be wrong to suggest that Shetland society remained unaltered from the early eighteenth century to the 1870s. Hance Smith is right to lay stress on the diversification of the economy during and after the Napoleonic Wars, especially the emergence of cod fishing, and the important part that Lerwick and its merchants played during the following decades. During this period there was – briefly – a loosening of the bonds of fishing tenure. But it was short-lived. Laurence Edmondston later wrote a racy account of the period:[308]

> Individuals [he said], who either could not or would not see the wisdom of this [fishing tenure] arrangement, in a certain state of society – entertaining theoretical views of political economy, suited only to great capital and high commercial civilization, – were unceasing in their denunciations against the landlords, as injuriously compelling their tenants to deliver to them their produce at a less price than they could obtain in the market, while the countervailing fact was overlooked, of the proportionally low rent paid for the land. This ad captandum argument was but too successful; the tenants became dissatisfied; many of them dishonestly eluded the compact by clandestine disposal of much of their produce to others than their masters, while these were paid with low rents, – and at length they demanded to be at liberty to give their labour to the highest bidder, and pay a higher money rent to their landlord as a receipt in full of all his annual claims on them. Several of the lairds, seduced by the specious but spurious simplicity of this free-trade view, annoyed by incessant and unjust charges of ignorance and oppression, or willing to be relieved from irksome details, consented, and the rest were soon compelled to follow, or have their lands untenanted.
>
> For a few years, all went on pretty smoothly; but the tenants had now fallen into the hands of a set of small shopkeepers, whose interest was not to secure their rents, or have regard to the permanent prosperity of the tenant, but to exhaust his means in shop advances; a result for which the system, rather than they, was to blame. Thus the tenants fell into habits of profusion and heavy arrears, and bad seasons supervening, the hollowness of the scheme at once became manifest. The shopkeepers (many of whom were also ruined) could not furnish supplies, because the tenants' substance and credit were exhausted; and the landlords, in want of their rents, were little able to relieve them. Some of them did, however, interpose nobly; and, but for their instrumentality, the tenants must in many instances have starved. The eyes of most people are now opened to the necessity of resuming the principle of the old system, which, in some instances, has been done, and already the aspect of things is improving.

Some of the merchants from the interregnum period themselves became merchant-lairds, with fishing tenure on their estates. James Hay, the progenitor of what became the most powerful merchant house in Shetland, Hay and Co., had argued

---

308. Laurence Edmondston, 'General observations on the county of Shetland', *The Statistical Account of the Shetland Islands,* Edinburgh and London 1841, pp.160-1.

forcibly in the 1780s that fishing tenure was inefficient and oppressive, and that government should abolish the link between tenure and fishing in the islands.[309] By the 1860s, however, Hay and Co. were lessees of four large Shetland estates, and the tenants on each of them were obliged to fish. On one of these estates, the Symbister estate in Whalsay, fishing tenure was still flourishing in its most primitive form as late as the 1860s. Speaking to a royal commission in 1872[310] an emigrant from Whalsay, William Stewart, recalled what he and his fellow-islanders had had to endure when he lived there, only ten years previously.

> The thing [he said] was carried on on a very strange system. Our land was put into us at a low rent, and our fish were taken from us at as low a value. The prices for the fish never varied, either for the spring or summer. Whatever they might be in the markets, they were all the same to us.

The commissioner asked: 'Did you not object to that?' Stewart replied: 'We had just to content ourselves with it, or leave the place.' And in his report the commissioner remarked that what we have here (albeit under the aegis of a merchant-lessee rather than a landlord) is Adam Smith's 1776 Shetland system 'in full vigour'.[311]

'I hope it will appear so faire and reasonable'

What did the parties in the share contracts make of their rights and obligations? We have some information about this question, from the very earliest days of fishing tenure.

On two occasions we find Shetland landlords pursuing their tenants before parochial bailie courts for what looks like comprehensive breach of their fishing contracts. In 1726 Thomas Gifford wrote what he called a 'remonstrance', to be read aloud in the bailie court of Northmavine, in which he lamented that his tenants had been selling their fish clandestinely to small traders. They 'are not ashamed', he marvelled, 'to act such knaveish and dishonest part'.[312] He didn't simply berate his tenants; he argued that everyone in the parish should be delivering their fish to him.

The arguments he used were moral ones. He pointed out that he had gone to 'vast charge and expence' to export the people's fish, and was tempted to give up doing so. But he offered to give them all one last chance. He urged them – his tenants and all the other parishioners – to sign an agreement to fish for him, at fixed prices, under a penalty of £6 per parcel of fish sold elsewhere.

> And as I have a natural right and power [he said] to oblige my own tenants to accept thereof, so I hope it will appear so faire and reasonable to all that no honest man in the paroch who other regairdeth his own interest or the publick good will refuse the same.

In the event 100 fishers, from almost every corner of the parish, signed Gifford's agreement.

I know of one other case where a landlord appealed to the bailie court to uphold the principle of fishing tenure. In 1743 Lady Mitchell, a landowner in the parish of

---

309. *Parliamentary Papers* 1785-1801, x, report, pp.25-8.
310. *Parliamentary Papers* 1872, xxxv, minutes of evidence, p.217.
311. *Parliamentary Papers* 1872, xxxv, report, p.4.
312. See Appendix, pp. 89-91, *infra*.

Sandsting and Aithsting, complained[313]

> that her haill tennents ... dispose off and sell their penny worths, such as fish, butter, oyle and slaughter beasts, etc., to other people, without giving her the first offer of the same, and is contrary to her agreement with them as tennants.

The court ordered the tenants to offer their produce to Lady Mitchell first, under the penalties contained in their leases; only if Lady Mitchell refused their offer were they at liberty to dispose of it as they wished.

Figure 25 A 'sixern' is setting off to the 'haaf' (deep-sea fishing) from the East Week, Fedeland, Northmavine, c.1890 (photograph by Jack Rattar). Fedeland was one of Shetland's main fishing stations. The fishers' temporary living quarters are in the background. *Copyright Shetland Museum*

These documents tell us two important things about fishing tenure. First, it is clear that in the earliest period, when the population of Shetland was recovering from the seventeenth century crises, landlords were not keen to evict valuable tenants. They appealed to law courts and mumbo-jumbo about the common weal instead. They had established the principles of fishing tenure, but they were chary about taking them to their final conclusion. No doubt the threat of eviction was normally sufficient.

---

313. Printed in the *Shetland Times*, 28 August 1897: the original document is not known to exist.

Secondly there is no evidence, even in the difficult years of the early eighteenth century, that the Shetlanders relished having to fish for their landlords. Later, George Low referred to the Shetlanders' 'vast grumblings' about their situation,[314] and James Gordon reported that they regarded themselves as 'the greatest slaves in nature'.[315] The fact that they never revolted doesn't imply that they were pleased with their lot. James C. Scott, in his fine work on share-croppers in Southeast Asia, warns us against assuming that lack of open rebellion means that a share-cropper is resigned to her destiny.[316] Scott writes at length about the share-croppers' favourite technique of, as he puts it, 'clandestinely improving their terms of exchange with landlords while avoiding open confrontations': that is, 'sell[ing] a portion of their crop before formal division of the harvest'. Shetland peasants as much as Burmese ones resorted to 'knaveish and dishonest' tricks, as Thomas Gifford put it, for as long as they were enmeshed in fishing tenure.

Faced with such stratagems the landowners were slightly unsure of their ground. Once again they occasionally brought miscreants to court; in one case as far as the Court of Session.[317] The small traders who bought the Shetlanders' fish, sometimes miles from shore, were called 'yaugers', and they appear to have been enterprising people. In 1792 one of them, James Hughson of Westsandwick, actually took two merchant-lessees to court himself, for harassment, and complained to the sheriff about what he called

> the feudal bondage which [the] tenants groan [under] and have been subjected to by the arbitrary conduct of their masters, which has well nigh brought these islands to ruin, and if continued will certainly terminate in the depopulation and misery of their inhabitants.[318]

Shetland landlords often found it difficult to defend their society, even to themselves. To make this even clearer I want to discuss a letter of 1761, written by a merchant-landlord in the island of Yell to a merchant in Unst who had just bought a small estate.[319] The letter, by Robert Neven of Windhouse, portrays beautifully the doubts and hesitations such men often felt. Neven's correspondent, William Mouat, had acquired a tiny fragment – one-ninth – of a township, whose tenant rented a much larger piece of land there from another landlord. Mouat had written to Neven asking if he, Mouat, would be justified in demanding a proportionate amount of the tenant's produce. This is what Neven said. 'You say right', he told Mouat,

> that its equitable when a tenant labours land of sundry proprietors, they should have a respective title to his product: but this is only upon a supposition that one individual by taking his land from the possessor rents his labouring.

In other words, there's a doubt in Neven's mind about the central fact of fishing

---

314. George Low, *A Tour through the Islands of Orkney and Schetland* [1774], Kirkwall 1879, p.120.
315. D.J. Withrington and I.R. Grant eds., *The Statistical Account of Scotland*, xix: *Orkney & Shetland*, Wakefield 1978, p.560.
316. James C. Scott, *The Moral Economy of the Peasant,* New Haven etc. 1976, p.231.
317. National Archives of Scotland, CS.271/60725: Andrew Scott of Greenwall v. Gilbert Robertson, 27 April 1810; Signet Library, Edinburgh 482:3 and 639:7: Scott v. Robertson.
318. Shetland Archives, SC 12/6/1792/8: Hughson versus Edmondston and others.
319. Shetland Archives, D.12/77.

tenure: the landlord's control of the tenant's labour. He goes on:

> But to say you or I should ask more than butter and cash for 2 merk undivided land out of 18 is a demand that wont be favoured in many places. If that land is always laboured and can nearly support one tenant your argument would be good; but in a contrary case its nothing.

He now becomes philosophical, in both senses of the word:

> Equety is a nice matter. We have all fix'd standards to it, tho' these are but rarely adher'd to in a primary sence. I dont know but it may bend that rule to make any further demand upon a labourer than ordinary landmails, ... and to oblidge them to other terms perhaps may have rather an arbitrary look. No man has a legal liberty of possessing one foot of your ground but upon your oun conditions, but if he can have a labouring independant of such (which is the present case in hand) you cant forse him in an equitable manner to hold it but upon his [terms].

This letter is extraordinarily revealing. Neven is worried that the landlords' actions may appear 'arbitrary', and advises Mouat against pressing the fishing tenure argument 'in a primary sence' – that is, to its logical conclusion. *Unless, that is, the landlord has the tenant entirely under her or his control.* Only when the tenant has no room for manoeuvre is it safe to be arbitrary.

Two things enabled the landlords to consolidate their position. First, by excambion and judicious purchases men like William Mouat eventually built up large, compact estates, whose tenants had to fish or leave. Secondly, the tenants, after subsistence crises like those of the 1770s, the 1780s, the early 1800s and the 1830s, became increasingly debt-bound, either at the landlords' own truck-shops or those of the landlords' lessees. As landlords and merchants became more and more confident about their role the tenants became increasingly cowed.

To show how submissive Shetlanders were I complete this section with an anecdote from the island of Whalsay. In 1889 an old man, Thomas Hutchison of Creediknowe, described for the Crofters Commission an event which had happened on the isle in his youth. The event had nothing to do with fair rents, but he still wanted to talk about it. One year, perhaps in the 1830s, the landlord had refused to take the tenants' fish, and Thomas and his colleagues decided to cure them themselves for sale elsewhere. The landlord heard about it, and summoned them to his pier at Symbister. When they got there the landlord's factor took the cured fish from them and cut each of them in two, making them unmarketable. '[We] got nothing for them', said Thomas. 'Not one farthing. Not one mite, and we went home with tears in our eyes to think we were such servants, and could not help ourselves'[320]

'Doubtful how far they are able to exercise any choice'

In 1872, following representations from some Shetland gentlemen, Sheriff William Guthrie went to the islands as a royal commissioner to investigate the truck-shops there. Guthrie was an extremely acute man, and he immediately began to investigate fishing tenure as well.

---

320. *Shetland Times*, 5 October 1889. For what may be a contemporary reference to this incident see the letter by 'Jecobas Herne' in the *Shetland Journal*, 1 May 1837.

'Complaints on this subject', he wrote,

> were made by tenants on the estates of Sumburgh and Quendale ... and on the island of Burra. It also appears ... that the obligation exists and is enforced on the estate of Lunna ...; on that of Ollaberry ...; on those of Mr Henderson, Mrs Budge, Messrs Pole & Hoseason ... ; in the island of Whalsay ... ; on the Gossaburgh estate ... ; and in Skerries. On other estates the tenants are nominally free, although it may some times be doubtful how far they are able to exercise any choice.[321]

Fishing tenure was as comprehensive as that. It thus becomes a mystery how it disappeared as rapidly as it did. We can dismiss immediately the notion, toyed with by some Shetland historians, that William Guthrie, or the government which appointed him, abolished fishing tenure. Clever as he was, Guthrie didn't dream of recommending anything so radical. Although he conceded that Shetland truck was 'due in no small degree to the habit of dependence, or submission, which the faulty relations between landlords and tenants have fostered', in the last analysis he did not regard himself 'at liberty to enter upon the land question ... as a substantive part of the enquiry'. 'I may at least', he concluded tentatively, 'be permitted to hope that, in any reform of the land tenancy laws of Scotland, the case of Shetland will not be forgotten'.[322]

Figure 26 A 'steeple' of fish at John Brown's station, Wadill Ayre, Burravoe, North Roe, in the late 1890s (photographer William A.S. Burgess). After the fish are gutted and salted they are dried in the sun on the stony beach; they are then built up into a stack. *Copyright Shetland Museum*

---

321. *Parliamentary Papers* 1872, xxxv, report, p.6.
322. *Parliamentary Papers* 1872, xxxv, report, p.56.

Throughout the centuries two historical forces have got to grips with peasant bondage in the world: markets and land reform. None of them is sufficient to deal with all the problems; in Shetland both combined in interesting ways to transform Shetland society. Market forces came first. A few years after Guthrie had departed, some merchants conducted experiments in fishing for herring around Shetland, using decked luggers. They were extremely successful, and in the early 1880s there was a period of massive growth in the new industry. There is no doubt that during this extremely brief period most Shetland estates dropped, almost simultaneously, the obligation for their tenants to fish. How the landlords made the decision, and how they conveyed it to their tenants, is at present more mysterious than the events in the early eighteenth century when fishing tenure was devised. No doubt the business relationship of the landlords themselves and their lessees with the new fishery was vital.

At the same time, Shetlanders seemed to experience a sort of revulsion against the subsistence agriculture of the townships, and the fishing techniques of the preceding era. Many of them flocked to Lerwick, or further afield, and a great fishing disaster in 1881 scunnered many of them with the small open boats which had been the mainstay of fishing tenure. When Lord Napier came to Shetland with his Crofters Commission, in 1883, hardly anyone spoke to him about truck or fishing tenure, except the inhabitants of Foula, the most isolated island.[323]

Robert Brenner, in an interesting footnote to an article on Neo-Smithian theories of development, asks why some societies found it relatively easy to move from peasant bondage into the modern world.[324] One of Brenner's examples is the peasant producer of industrial crops, without sufficient land to provide her with means of subsistence: *mutatis mutandis*, the Shetland tenant of the eighteenth and nineteenth century.[325] Brenner calls modes of production like this 'transitional', because 'they allow for a *more or less* direct transition to formally capitalist class relations and co-operative labour under the pressures of competition on the market'.

I don't want to suggest that the herring fishery solved the Shetlanders' problems. Less than a decade after the beginning of the boom there was an equally remarkable slump, from about 1886 to 1896. During those years the Shetlanders who hadn't gone to Lerwick – and of course there were thousands of them – got to grips with the problems of their land tenure. Fishing tenure had gone, but rural Shetlanders still had pressing problems: in particular, their insecurity of tenure, and the chronic debt which was an apparently inextinguishable aspect of life in the islands. The debt was of course getting more onerous during the depression. The crofting legislation of 1886 had been enacted just in time to assist the Shetlanders; there were more fair rent applications per head in Shetland than in any other part of Scotland.

Sheriff Brand of the Crofters Commission presided over tribunals in Shetland in 1889 and 1892, delighting the Shetlanders with his decisions and discomfiting the landlords. It is not too much to say that the events of the decade from 1886 to 1896, *in spite* of the depression, cured the psychological wounds inflicted on the

---

323. *Parliamentary Papers* 1884, xxxiii, minutes of evidence, pp.1355ff.
324. Robert Brenner, 'The origins of capitalist development: a critique of Neo-Smithian Marxism', *New Left Review*, no. 104, 1977, p.52n.
325. Another good example, incidentally, would be the women knitters in Lerwick, who knitted with wool provided by local hosiery merchants. Such women were enmeshed in truck until the Second World War.

Shetlanders by fishing tenure. In 1897 the herring fishing picked up again, and by 1905 the industry was booming beyond the Shetlanders' wildest expectations. Shetlanders felt secure in their tenurial relationships, and secure, for the time being, in their economic ones.

'Not entirely under capitalists'

I conclude by asking a question which Adam Smith failed to ask. Was Shetland in the eighteenth and nineteenth centuries a civilised society? It is not an easy question to answer if we aren't precise and honest about the society's essential characteristics.

Shetland's critics, mainly educated men and women from outside the islands, were fairly hopeless scourges. They railed against fishing tenure in an extremely abstract way, and they failed to galvanise the Shetlanders into action, because they uttered their complaints in pamphlets and books.

Those who replied to them, the Shetland landlords and merchants, had many advantages. They knew their society intimately. They could point to their tenants' docility, and interpret it not as cowed dependence, as the moralisers did, but as pure contentment. When truck and tenure were under fierce attack in the 1870s, merchants and landlords combined to argue that they were a great success. William Irvine, a partner in Hay and Co., compared rural Shetland favourably with the great British cities. Shetlanders, he said

> are, without doubt, more independent and less undercontrol than mechanics ... (who are obliged to work under a stated number of hours every day), and consequently are more happy and contented. We have no international societies in Shetland. ... For my own part I would ten times rather live a year in a Shetland cottage, surrounded by pure air, than a week in one of the slums of London or Glasgow.[326]

To grasp precisely what Irvine really wanted to say about fishing tenure, but refrained from saying, I find it useful to listen to yet another commentator, one of few from outside Shetland who spoke out in favour of the islands' political economy. John MacCulloch, a chemist and geologist who visited Shetland in the 1820s, sympathised deeply with the landlords who entertained him, and poured scorn on the 'ultraphilanthropists', as he styled their critics.[327] MacCulloch's analysis of Shetland society, at once shrewd and eccentric, was as follows.

Shetland, he said, 'is a fishing country',

> ... not entirely under capitalists who employ them for money wages but under capitalists who have little money and much [uncultivatable] land. ... Therefore, the landowner, who cannot live by his land rent, on account of the inevitable poverty of his tenants from their numbers and the subdivision of the land, must pay the fisherman wages in lots of land.

Adam Smith's rents from the sea are startling enough; wages paid in land are more startling still.[328] MacCulloch went on:

---

326. *Parliamentary Papers* 1872, xxxv, minutes of evidence, p.84.
327. Derek Flinn, *Travellers in a Bygone Shetland*, Edinburgh 1989, p.220.
328. But cf. A.F. Robertson, *The Dynamics of Productive Relationships: African share contracts in comparative perspective*, Cambridge 1987, p.269: 'does the supply of labour [in share-cropping] constitute a "rent", or is the supply of land services a "wage"?'.

> Surely, Shetland tenants, an it please you to call them so, are better off than Highland tennants. ... They are better off than labourers elsewhere. They need never want work – they may always have house and land – catch fish when they choose to go out, marry, rear families and die at home instead of in a workhouse. They are not turned out of their farms if they choose to continue and do their duty, and if they choose not, why then they find a pleasure ... it is to be presumed in want or grumbling. If the farm and fishing produce no surplus the landlord takes no rent till it does – if it produces nothing he feeds them till they can feed themselves and repay him from the next harvest. Where is the labourer who can do that? Consider them as labourers and thre[e] fourths of their time to themselves, and their lot is admirable.

Irvine and MacCulloch imagined that the Shetlanders had lots of *choice*, more of it than almost everyone else. Both of them argued that the landowners and merchants were so benevolent that no self-respecting tenant would dream of neglecting what MacCulloch calls 'their duty'.

There is not much, in my opinion, to say in favour of a society like this. There were no choices. Remember what William Stewart said to Sheriff Guthrie in 1872: 'We had just to content ourselves with it, or leave the place.' The reason that there were no choices is that, as Brenner says, the Shetlanders had no direct access to their own means of subsistence. To people like Irvine and MacCulloch, both of them committed to private property, that state of affairs wasn't the problem at all. To a historian it should be central.

Shetland fishing tenure was a species of that regrettably common state in the history of the world called peasant bondage, in this case an amalgam of share tenancy and debt-bondage.[329] The crises of the seventeenth century catapulted most Shetlanders from a relatively free state into a relatively unfree one. They got land and credit, as the apologists pointed out, but they had to give, they were 'bound' to give, their labour in exchange.

There is nothing particularly complex about this society, or the way its landlords extracted their (very visible) surplus. While I was writing this chapter I noticed a review by George Kerevan of Gramsci's *Prison Notebooks*, where Kerevan listed the manifold modes of production and power in the pre-modern Mediterranean south:

> semi-feudal latifundia, mercantile capitalism, Bourbonist absolutism, tribalism, the independent cosmopolitan power of the Catholic church; all infused with the remnants of Classical culture.[330]

By contrast Shetland of the eighteenth and nineteenth centuries was a rather straightforward place, whose inhabitants were suspended in a dreary and long drawn-out transition between old and new worlds.

---

329. I borrow this classification from Judith Ennew, *Debt Bondage: a survey*, London 1981, pp.69-70.
330. George Kerevan, review in *Chapman*, no. 58, 1989, p.83.

Appendix: Documents

1. The letter of 1299 about Papa Stour

Allum þeim mannum sem þetta bref sia eða heyra senda allir logðingismenn af hiatlandi. Qveðiu. Guðs. ok sina þat se yðr kunnikt at a þui are er liðit uar burd uars herra iesu xristi. m⁰. cc⁰. xc⁰. ok ix⁰. uetr. let herra þor ualldr þoris. son. bera uitni fyr oss a logþingi. orð þau sem ragnhilldr simunar. dottir. hafði talat. baro þeir sua uit ni Juar bondi aeiði ok haralldr iborgarfirði at þeir uoro hia þui istofvni ahertogabœnvm ipapey manadagenn idymbildaga uiku er Ragnhilldr tok sua til orða at breka sætr uar ecki ileigu með skat jorðu upiihu si ok hertogin skylldi taka fulla leigo þot breka sætr uæri ecki með. en þorualldr sagði. her hafa sua margir goðir menn um uellt sem var þorkell inesi herra Eirikr Sigurðr erkidiakn herra Eindriði ok margir aðrir dugan di menn þeir er hafðo umboð mins herra hertogans huilika landskylld þeir toko hanom til handa i papey. fyr mer. Ragn hilldr suaraði. ek œnti ecki Eindriða œrum. er hann líop ustan or noregi ok uissi alldri fagnat. en þer allir sem uissuð þa hafa suikit hertogann. en sueinn prestr ok halfdan abruarsætri baro sua at þeir uoro hia þui ummorgonen eftir atysdagenn uti ituninu a fyrsagdum bœ er Ragnhilldrsagði sua til herra þorualldar at þu skal't ecki uera minn iudás. þot þu ser hertogans ok þessi orð uitnadi herra þorualldr aalla þa sem nær uoro. Profaz ok alldri meiri uerðavrar a allri papey en sua sem iafnan hefir gengit at fyrnd. mork gullz brendri með uelltu iorðu huert penings land. en ilandskylld halfs annars mælis uerð af huerri mork brendri ok er þa .ij. salld ahueriv penings landi. Nu af þui at herra þorvalldr ok þeir fleiri sem hon hafði til talat . uilia ganga logligri dul fyr sialfum hertoga num. þa gafvm ver þetta rannzaks bref til uars uirðulegs herra hertogans um fyr sogd malefni. ok þui at uer hofdum eigi logþinngis insigli þa settu þessir af uarum kumpanum sin insigli fyr þetta bref til sannz uit nis burdar. herra Eirikr ungi. Gregorius bendictz. son. Juar sperra Magnus hogna. son. Erlendr geirmundar. son. gunni agnipum. Erlendr alfeitr.

To all the men who see or hear this letter, all the lawthingmen of Shetland send God's greeting and their own. Be it known to you that, in the year when 1299 winters had passed from the birth of our Lord Jesus Christ, Sir Thorvald Thoreson had testimony brought before us at the lawthing [concerning] the words spoken by Ragnhild Simunsdottir.

Ivar, 'bondi' of Aith, and Harald in Burrafirth, bore witness that they were present in the 'stofa' of the ducal farm in Papa, on Monday in Passion Week, when Ragnhild spoke, saying that Bragister wasn't rented out as part of the 'scat land' of the house, and the duke should take full rent even though Bragister were not included. But Thorvald said: 'So many good men have dealt with this – such as Thorkell in Nes, Sir Eirik, Archdeacon Sigurd, Sir Eincrid, and many other able men who had full authority from my lord the duke concerning the sort of rent they took for him in Papa formerly'. Ragnhild answered: 'I gave no heed to the mad Eindrid, who ran away from Norway here and never knew a day's happiness; but all of you who knew have deceived the duke'.

But Svein the priest and Halfdan of Brouster bore witness that they were present the next morning, on Tuesday, out in the 'toon' of the aforesaid farm, when Ragnhild said to Sir Thorvald: 'You shan't be my Judas, though you be Judas to the duke'. Sir

Thorvald called all those present as witnesses of these words.

[Herewith] it is also demonstrated that there [has] never [been] greater payment from the whole of Papa than that which has been common from of old: there is a mark of burnt gold for every cultivated 'pennyland', and in rent 1½ 'mælar' from every mark burnt, and there are then 2 'sáld' on every 'pennyland'.

Now, since Sir Thorvald and the others she had spoken to wish to swear a legal oath of denial [about Ragnhild's accusations] before the duke himself, we gave this letter of enquiry to our noble lord the duke about the aforesaid matters, and since we had no lawthing seal the following of our companions set their seals on this letter by way of confirmation: Sir Eirik Ungi, Gregorius Benedictson, Ivar Sperra, Magnus Hognason, Erlend Geirmundson, Gunni of Gnipum, Erlendr Alfeit.

Arnamagnæan Institute, Copenhagen 100, 3. The transcription of the text is by Paul Bibire.

2. *Obligation by John Tulloch of Fiblister to Robert Sinclair of Quoyin, 1626.*

Be it kend till all men be thir presentis, me Johne Tulloch, thrid lawfull sone of umquhill Thomas Tulloch of Feblesetter, proprieter of tua merk half merk land thair, tuelff pennye the merk, for certane guid causes onerous and consideratiounes moveing me, my awin will, utilitie and profeit foirsein and considerit, and for sindrie gratitudis and guid deidis done to me be my weilbelovit brother in law Robert Sinclair of Quoyin, and specialie for fulfilling the will and command of the said umquhill Thomas my father, to be bund and oblist, lykas I be thir presentis faithfullie promitt, bind and oblis me and my airis, in nawayis to sell, annailie, dispone, delapidat nor put away the said tua merk half merkland in Feblesetter nor pertinentis thairof, nor na part of the same, nor na utheris my landis nor heritagis fallen or belanging to me, ather be deceis or dispositioun of my said umquhill father, or that may fall or belang to me, ather be deceis or be dispositioun of quhatsumever of my bretherine, to na maner of persone nor persones in tymecuming, without the speceall advyse, consent and assent of the said Robert Sinclair and his airis or assignis first haid and obtenit thairto; and if it salhappin me or my airis to have ado with moneyis or uther guds equivalent thairto, sa that we salhappin to be straitit or urgeit to sell, annaly or awayput the saidis landis or utheris foirsaidis that sall pertein to us or ony part thairof, at any tyme heirefter, than and in that caise I bind and oblis me and my foirsaidis to mak the first offer and to sell, annailie and dispone the same to the said Robert Sinclair and his foirsaidis, for the lyk and selfsame conditiounes and lands pryce as the lyk landis of rentaill within the contrey hes bein and is in use to be sauld for, according to the ald pryces of the said countrie of Yetland, viz. tuentie four gulyeounes for the merk land, tuelf pennyes the merk, aughtein gulyeounes for the merk, ix d. the merk, tuelf gulyeounes for the merk land, sex d. the merk, etc.

And if it salhappin me or my foirsaids to do in the contrair heirof the said Robert or his foirsaidis being willing and hable to accept of and fulfill the saidis conditiounes, than and in that caise quhatsumever alienatioun, deid or dispositioun that salhappin to be done be me or my foirsaidis in defame heirof, I be thir presentis willis and consent the samen be declairit null of nane availl, force nor effect, nor nawayis miscal nor mak fayth in judgement nor outwith the samen in tymecuming, and it to be lesum to the said Robert and his foirsaidis to offer and delyver the saidis landis pryces and availlis to me and my foirsaidis, and incaise of refuisall to consigne the samen in the handis of the bailie or minister of the parochine of Northmaven, or any landit gentlemanes hand within the samen being responsall for the tyme, and thairefter he and his foirsaidis to have full and frie ingress, access and entrie to the saidis landis, and I and my foirsaidis oblist to mak, perfyte, subscryve and delyver to the said Robert and his foirsaidis suffycient evidentis, chartours and infeftmentis thairupoun, in dew and competent forme, with all clauses requisite to the making, perfyteing, subscriving and delyvering of the quhilkis to the said Robert and his foirsaidis, [and] I be the tennour heirof, now as than and than as now astrict, bind and obleise me and my foirsaidis, and for the mair securitie I am content and consentis thir presentis be registrat in the buikis of counsall, sheref or commissar bukis of Orkney and Shet[land], to have the strenth of ane decreit with executoriallis neidfull to be direct thairupoun on a simple charge of sex dayis allanerlie; and heirto contitutis [*blank*] my [*tora*] *promitten de rato* etc., in witnes quhairof, writtin be Patrik Sandis, notar publict, subscrivit with my h[and] as followis, my seill is affixit as Feblesetter the elevint day of Marche Jaj VJc tuentie sex yeiris, befoir thir witnesses: Scipio Bruce of Ure, Andro Tulloch my brother, Gilbert Robertsone, tailyeour, Mans Robertsone in Hougoland, John Cromertie and Mans Gifhart, servitouris to the said Patrik. ...

National Archives of Scotland, RD.11/204, reg. 6 July 1630. The registered version is in RD.1/432, folios 310-11.

3. Extract from rental of Shetland of c.1628: notes anent Shetland weights, measures and values.

Anent the weyghts, measures and rekningis of the dewties of Yetland

Ane cuttell wodmell is a Zelandis elne, pryce thairof is 4s. Scottis. Sex cuttellis is a shilling wodmell and ten shilling wodmell is a pak. Ane d. leanger is payable be ane calf skin or half cuttell wodmell, or pryce thairof 2s.

Ane d. butter is 4 merk butter, sex pennyis butter makis ane leispund, tuelf leispund makis a barrell butter. The pryce of the leispund is 48s.

Ane can oyllie is the measure of a Scottis quart, pryce thairof in the countrey 12s. 4 cannis makis ane bull and 9 bullis makis ane barrell oyllie.

Aught ures of land makis ane merk of land, 18 merk land makis ane last of land, and 4 lastis of land is a peice of corneteynd.

Ane last land being 18 merk payis 6 meillis, viz. 3 leispund butter, 3 bullis oyllie.

Whair the corneteynd is payit in packit guidis ilk peice corneteynd is ane barrell butter ane yeir and ane barrell oyllie another yeir.

Ilk Yetland shilling is 2 meillis, quhairof j meill payit in butter and another in oyllie.

Ilk meill of scat is j leispund butter or j bull oyllie.

National Archives of Scotland, E.41/7, folio 2. These notes may have been compiled by Andro Smyth, who was from time to time servant of the king's tacksman in Shetland. The document is certainly in Smyth's hand.

4. Extract from rental of Shetland of c.1628: land-rent and scat paid by townships and districts in Bressay.

Brassay landmeallis

| Wodmell | Butter |

Kircabuster ½ merk, vj d. merk: j cuttell ½ cuttell, j d. ob. [Allegeit 8d. merk *in margin*]
Hoversta iij merk, viij d. merk: viij cuttell, j leispund ij d.
Keldabuster vj merk ij ures, ix d. merk: iij s. j cuttell, iij leispund j d.
Hewgone iiij merk, vj d. merk: viij cuttell, j leispund ij d.
Gunyelsta iiij merk ½, viij d. merk: ij s., ij leispund.
[Allegeit 8d. merk *in margin*] Aith ij last of land: ij pakis, j barrell butter.
Seatter iiij merk ½, viij d. merk: ij s., ij leispund.

Brassay scat

| Wodmell | Butter and oyllie |

[Reteinit thair *in margin*] Kircabuster: iiij s., iiij d. leanger, iiij meillis. Reteinit ij cuttell [and] 3 pert d. leanger thairof be the minister for his gleib, and ij d.
Brugh: iiij s., iiij d. leanger, iiij meillis.
Hoversta: iiij s., iiij d. leanger, iiij meillis. [Reteinit *in margin*] Reteinit thairof ij cuttell be the minister for his gleib, and ij d.
Keldabuster: iiij s., iiij d. leanger, iiij meillis.
Hewgone and Gunilsta: iiij s., iiij d. leanger, iiij meillis.
[Reteinit *in margin*] Culbensburcht: iiij s., iiij d. leanger, iiij meillis. Reteinit thairof iij cuttell [and] ½ d. leanger be the minister for his gleib, and j d. ob.
Noss and Nosssound: vj s., vj d. leanger.

National Archives of Scotland, E.41/7, folio 4. This short extract deals with the 'landmeallis' (land-rent) and 'scat' (tax) paid by townships and districts in the small island of Bressay. Most of the seven scat-paying districts paid four 'shillings' of 'wodmell' (cloth), four 'meillis' of butter and oil, and four 'pennies' of an extra scat called 'leanger'. Some of the scat was 'reteinit' to provide a glebe for the minister, and the township of Aith paid no scat at all: Earl Patrick Stewart had given it to Captain Thomas Knichtsoun in 1593 (John H. Ballantyne and Brian Smith eds., *Shetland Documents 1580-1611*, Lerwick 1994, no. 207). The crown owned parts of some of the townships in the districts; these lands therefore paid land-rent to the king. Each mark of land rented in this way paid six, eight or nine 'pennies' per mark in rent, in cloth and butter.

An example: Hoversta paid the normal amount of scat. We know from Gifford's rental of 1716 (National Archives of Scotland, RH.9/15/176, p.23) that Hoversta comprised 36 marks of land. Three of the 36 marks of land belonged to the king, and each of the three paid eight 'pennies' in rent: 3 x 8 = 24 pennies, paid as eight ells of cloth (16 pennies) plus one lispund two pennies of cloth (8 pennies).

5. Description of the scattald marches of Yell, 1667.

The description of the merches of the severall scattells in the island of Yell, according as they were fund to be boundit, the tyme when they were surveyed by me, Gilbert Niven, baillie of the said isle, which was begun upon the 27th day of Marche 1667 yeires, being accompanied by the persons after named, or the most of them, at the severall merches, who did all agree thereto and aprove the bounding thereof, conform to the description therof, in manner underwreattin: they are to say Androw Fraser, portioner of North Seatter, William Henderson, portioner of Gloupe, Magnus Mansone there, David Spence, portioner of Houlland, James Spence of Midbreck, Andrew Hendriesone and James Fraser, portioners of Brughe, James Spence in Turfhous, Ninian Hendersone of Gardie, James Nisbit, portioner of Kunningsetter, Piter Nisbit in Sellofirth, Magnus Ollavesone, Peter Donaldsone, Androw

Bartilsone, portioners of Basta, Androw Edmonstoun of Hascosea, Androw Johnsone and Osea Johnsone, portioners of Houll and Camb, Osea Scott, portioner of Reafirth, Francis Johnsone, portioner of Awick, Lawrence Tyrie of Quoyon, John Sinclair of Gossabrugh, Arnold and Antony Mansones, portioners of Nebeback, Robert Petersone, portioner of Hamnavo, Daniel Erasmussone, portioner of Arisdaill, Thomas Mathewsone and John Petersone, portioners of Coppasetter, Magnus Mathewson, portioner of Ulsta, Robert Irving, portioner of Seatter, Laurence Garthsone, portioner of Nether Houll, Daniell Hawick, portioner of South-Ledie, with many other witnesses who were present.

HOULLAND SCATTELL, being the first northmost scattell, is bounded to the west and north with the sea, to the east and south with Brugh scattell and the sea. The first merche-merk devyding these scattells stands upon the tope of the litle hill or Hillock be-east the litle peice of dyke, which is builded from the north end of the locke or water besyd the kirk of North Yell, to the head of the gooe at the north sea banks (called commonlie Dyelda-gooe), upon which hillock be-east the said peice of dyke as said is, ther hes ancientlie been (as it seemes), a ward or watch place is to be fund; the first divyding marche stone standing neir-about in the midle of the waist ground between the dykis of Houlland and Brughe, acknowledged to be from the said watch-place, the second marche stone, from which stone the lyn of the merche was fund to goe straight to a great flatt stone which lyes at the distance of ane pair of butts or therby, from the northmost crooke or bught of the ancient hill dykes between Houlland and Brughe, which by the consent of all present was fund to be a merche stone, and accordinglie was renewed by laying a heape of stones upon it, from which merche the merche goes to the hill or hillock called Houlna-houl, and from that the lyne of the merche inclyning a little more westward to the hill or hillock called the westmost Mossa-houle, which was by all foresaid acknowledged to be a merche, and was renewed by rearing an heape of stones upon it. From thence to the head of the myre called Kininga-loighe or the devyding myre, and from the foot of that with a straight lyne to the litle hill or hillock called Faugla-feyll, and from that to a great flatt rock (which is called the Heilla) lying at the south syd of the slack called Marka or Merkeiesmoode at the Neip or west sea banks, which is the last and westmost merche poynting out the south-most bounds of the scattell of Houlland, and the north-most of the scattell of Brughe.

BRUGHE SCATTELL is the second boundit the north part with the sea, and west and north with Houlland sc[at]tell as is, and then the rest of it both to the west and east is boundit by the sea, and to the south with Sandwick scattell. The first merche mark devyding between it and Sandwick scattell is a conspicuous merche-stone with stones sett about it for supporters, at the west Neip or sea banks, upon the north syd of the weik called Brawick, from whence the merche l[yes ea]st and south, with a straight lyne to that place of the hill above and benorth Sellafirth (called Markins Houle or the merche hillock), where a merche stone stands which is not verie conspicuous, nor could the merche at that time be gottin maid more manifest, becaus ther are no stones therabout, onlie the sure mark to know that merche infaliblie by is, that when you stand besyd it the kirk or chapell which stands in the town of Gudsher, will apeare from that place to stand as if it stood at the foot of the hill which lyes west and north from that town. From which merche of Merkins-houle the lyne of the merche goes to the east sea-banks, at the strype or litle burne runing down without the north-most garth dykes of Sandwick into the sea, at the place called Mill-goe, ther being no other merche at the east sea banks to distinguish between these scattells but the said strype or burne. And this according to the foresaid discription is the south bound of Brughe scattell, and the north bound of Sandwick scattell.

SANDWICK SCATTELL is boundit as said is to the north with Brughe scattell, to the west and east with the sea on both syds (except soe much as by the following discription will be fund to be boundit to the west with Windhous scattell), on the south it is partlie boundit by Windhous and partlie by Reafirth scattell. The first merk devyding between Sandwick and Windhous scattell is to be fund at the west Neip or sea banks, wher ther hes ancientlie been a peice [of] dyke builded with stones neirest the sea banks, and farthest from it (as it seemes) builded with failles and stones together, which peice of dyke is called Eners-gord. The lyne of the merche goes east and south, as the said peice of dyke steeth poynts to a peice of ground, which (as it [see]mes) has ancientlie been dyked about, and as it is said been manured and dwelt upon (which is called Beneserge), the lyne of the merche lying without that part of the dyke steith which surrounds it towards the north, without which dyke steith and towards the north as said is, there lyes a litle loch (or pool rather), between which and the said dyke steith the lyne of the merche goes (the said Beneserge lying close to it within Windhouse scattell, upon the right hand as ye goe from the west to the east), east and south to the brow of the hill which lyes west and south from Dasetter, in sight of Basta vo, and then it turnes south by the descent of that hill, and in the descent down towards the burne (commonlie called the burne of Colvasetter) ther stands some stones which seemed (but could not be certanlie determined) to be merche stones. The line of the merche going over the burne a muskit shott or therby beneath and be-east the loch, out off the which the forsaid burne proceeds (which loche lyes in Windhous scattell), and soe the lyn of the merche goes by the ascent of the hill be-south the said burne, haveing Sandwick scattell on the left hand, and Windhous on the right, southwards by the ridge of the hill, to the highest ryse or promontor therof, to the know or hillock called Trullakeldaes-houle. From the which place of Trullakeldaes-houle the lyne of the merche goes east and south with a straight lyne, having yet Sandwick scattell on the left hand, and Reafirth scattell on the right, to the south end of the loch or water called Siglara-vatten, out of the which ther runs a burne into the sea called Marca-mudes-vo, which burne is the onlie merche at the east sea banks, divyding between the scattells of Sandwick and Reafirth, and this, according to the former discription, bounds Sandwick scattell to the west and south, partlie with the sea, and the rest Windhous and Reafirth scattells, being boundit to the east always with the sea.

WINDHOUS SCATTELL is bounded on the north and east, according to the former description, with Sand-wick [sca]ttell, till it come to the said place or hillock called Trulla-keldaes-houle, from whence the lyne of the merch comes south along the ridge of the great hill be-east the house of Windhous, and down by the descent therof, having alwise Reafirth on the left hand, Windhous scattell on the right, at the foot of which hill to the south, in the westmost creik of Reafirth Vo, ther are two boates nousts between which there stands a conspicuous merch stone (the eastmost noust belonging to Reafirth, and the other to Windhous scattell), from which merch stone the lyne of the merche goes up by the ascent of the hill, south and west, to the south end of the loch which lies besouth Seatter, called Vandringa-Vatten (becaus the lyne of the merche which devyds Reafirth to the east from Windhous scattell, goes nearest south through the middle of that loch) and in the brow or ascent of the hill besouth the said loche, ther is a merche stone sett up with stones about it, from which the lyne of the merche goes southwards along the hill, to the knoues or hillocks called Unna-Stakaes-Houla, wher stands a great stone. acknowledged to be the southmost merche poynting out the bounds of Reafirth scattell to the west [*rectius* east], and Windhous scattell to the east [*rectius* west], from the which stone the lyne of the merche goes east and south, having Reafirth scattell on the left hand and Ottersweick on the right, to the slack upon the great hill which comes south from Reafirth, called Sturascord, on the north side wherof ther stands a merche stone from whence the lyne of the merche goes streight a little benorth the north dyke of Quoyon, and soe from thence to a place at the sea-banks called Lamba-hifda, wher ther stands a verie conspicuous merche stone, which is the eastmost merche bounding Reafirth scattell to the south, and Ottersweick scattell to the north.

REAFIRTH SCATTELL as manifestlie apeares by the discription above is boundit to the north with Sandwick scattell, to the east with the sea, and to the west and south with Windhous and Ottersweick scattells.

OTTERSWICK SCATTELL is boundit to the north as said is, with Reafirth scattell, haveng its westmost border from the said great stone which stands besyd Unna-Stacks-houlla, with a straight lyne southward to the warth or watche-place which stands upon the tope of the great hill besouth Sturascord called Moe-feyll, from which warth or watcheplace the south border of that scattell, and the north border of Nebeback scattell goes down with a straight lyne to the east sea-banks, wher stands a verie manifest merche besyd the gooe called Markina-gooe, or the merchegooe. And this conform to the above wreattin discription poynts out the bounds and merches of that scattell.

NEBEBACK SCATTELL is boundit to the north with Ottersweick scattell, as said is, and to the east and south with the sea, the west border therof going down from the said wart or watcheplace upon Moe-feyll southwards to. the head or place where the great burne of Aresdaill seems to have its beginning, which burne runing from thence to the sea bounds the said scattell to the west [*rectius* east], and Ulsta scattell to the east [*rectius* west].

ULSTA SCATTELL being bounded to the east by Nebeback scattell, and the burne of Arisdaill forsaid, has its north border bounded by a burne which runs from the west, and falls into the said burne of Arisdaill, called Viga-dales-wo, and from the head of that burne the lyne of the merche goes west and south to the tope of the hill above Seatter in South Yell, called the Warth of Seatter, and from that warth the lyne of the merche goes down west to the burn which is between Seatter and Cloden, called Mae-da dales-woe, or the burne in the merche-dale. And by the forsaid discription the east and north border of Ulsta scattell, or Cata-hala, as it is ancientlie called (it being alwayes bounded on the south by the sea) and the west border therof which is the east border of Strand scattell is poyntit out.

STRAND SCATTELL being partlie bounded to the south and east by Ulsta scattell, has its bounds to the north by a straight lyne coming from the head of the said burne of Arisdaill, westward and benorth the said burne called Viga-dales-woe, and goes to the southmost end and highest part of the great hill lying upon the north syd of the great slack or valley called Noube, from whence againe the lyne of the merche goes straight to ane stone merche standing at the sea-banks between Brughe and Westsandwick, besyd the gooe called Merkies-gooe, soe that this discription poynts out the east, north and west border of Strand scattell, and the south border of Westsandwick scattell.

WEST-SANDWICK SCATTELL being bounded as said with Strand scattell to the south, and alwise to the west by the sea, comes for its east border with a straight lyne from the brow of the said great hill, benorth Noube (wher Strand scattell terminates to the north and to the west), and goes north with a straight lyne along the westmost syd of that hill, till it comes to some great stones lying in the way, which comes fra West-Sandwick to Holsagarth (which stones are weill knowen, being called Hillono-whida), from which stones called Hillono-whida, the north border of Sandwick scattell, and the south of Graveland scattell, goes westward with a straight lyne to the sea-banks, at a place called Bowagardie, towards the south syd therof, upon a piece of ryseing ground ther stands a conspicuous merche.

GRAVELAND SCATTELL being boundit to the south, as haith been said, with Sandwick scattell, is boundit all along to the west and north from the said merche at Bowagardie by the sea, and to the east it is bounded by a lyne comeing neirlie north from the said stones or stoney place, called Hellono-whida by the ridge of the hill lying between Raga and Gremesta to a certane poynt at the sea-banks weill knowen by the name of Scarva-tonga, which is the eastmost sea-bank merche of Graveland scattell, and the west merche of that part of Windhouse scattell, which lyes besouth and westward from Windhouse, soe that the north part of Windhous scattell lying benorth Seatter is boundit all along by the sea to the west, and to the north and east with Sandwick and Reafirth scattill, and continues to be boundit in the south part therof by Reafirth, Otterswick, and Nebeback scattell to the east, and to the south with Strand scattell, only it is to be knowen that benorth the lyne of Strand scattell, which goes from the head of the burne called the burne of Arisdaill to the face of the hill benorth Noube, as is above descrybed, ther is waist ground not stricklie merched, which is ancientlie called Hollmennis-hogga or vo [blank] hill wherin all the scattellers of Strand and Nebeback may as farelie pasture as any in Windhous scattell may do.

And this is the true description of the bounding of the forsaid scattells, as they wer fund to lie and to be boundit, conforme to the above wreatten discription in all poynts. In witnes wherof and of the trouth of the haill premises, in soe far as it was possible to determine the same, I have wreattin and subscribit this present discription and declaration, this twintie fourth day of Apryll Jaj VJc and sixtie seven yeires.

(s.s) Gilbert Nieven, baillie of Yell.

The original is not known to exist. The above transcript (Shetland Archives, SC.12/50/1) is by Thomas Irvine (1790-1877). He writes in a docket: 'The description of the scathold marches of Yell from which this copy was made is in the handwriting of Gilbert Nieven of Windhouse, baillie of Yell, and written upon five sheets of stout foolscap paper joined together with paste, edge upon edge in continuation, so that the whole forms a roll of six feet in length and fourteen inches in breadth, with a margin two inches wide. The manuscript is whole and complete (save one word), and the character large, distinct and well written. It was lately in possession of the family of Gossaburg, but now in the possession of Mr Gilbert Duncan, N.P., Lerwick, who allowed me to take a copy of it, which I wrote upon common paper at Lerwick June 14th 1821; afterwards I wrote this copy on parchment at Midbrake, December 28th 1821. T. Irvine.'

6. Division of Ure, Eshaness, 1688.

This is the just divisione off my twenty eight merks land in Ure, how it sould be laboured yierly, the one thrid to bear, ane other thrid to oats and the other thrid ley, swa that the [merks *deleted*] equall thrid pairt lyeth ley yierly tow about, everie thrid being alyke good.

Oat land in 1688	The whole Garth is of pisses is The Easter Great Gerdistrengs is The Great Custahoulls is The Frustrenge is The Soverlies is The Four Belaribs is The Muerastrengs is	5 2 2 1 2 2 1	
Bear land in 1688	The Quyes is of pissis is Brunsdeald is Guddateake The Ferlies is Skoeteake and the rige att the goe is Hallinkine and Gunnateake is The Cups is Eallenadeald is Liascolldeald and Lawsdeald is Susastreng and Fealsteake is The Dealls at Liascoll is The Float beneath Liascoll is	2 1 1 1 1 1 1 1 1 1 1 3	This way is noe wayes to be altered, it being equally casten and proven to be right and good for the behove off corn and fodder, neyther is ther any more to be broken owt from grasse or middeu withowt hurt to both. James Oliphant
The ley land in 1688	The Litell Gerdistrengs is of pisses Maimateake and Litell Cussahowll is The Waster Great Gerdistrengs is The Howlls att Liascoll is The Tuptalands is The Groath is The Roerdealds is The Siladisks is The Kirk Strengs is The Breadelds is	2 1 3 1 2 1 1 1 1 2	

Shetland Archives, GD.144/48/22. A crop-rotation of this kind must have been unique in seventeenth century Shetland. The lands were 'equally casten': this seems to mean that they were 'thrown' into three divisions (*Oxford English Dictionary*, 'cast', 46a), each of which contained 15 'pisses'. James Oliphant possessed 20 marks land in Ure, 18 marks land in Liascoill and 12 marks land in Northhouse, 'all lyand in the said towne of Ure', paying nine, six and six 'pennies' of rent respectively (National Archives of Scotland, RS.44/4 folios 234-6). These lands comprised the whole of Ure. Perhaps the 45 'pisses' in Oliphant's scheme, composed of 29 named rigs or blocks of rigs, were 45 marks of land, equalised to pay eight 'pennies' per mark each.

7. 'Remonstrance by Thomas Gifford of Busta to and agreement with the inhabitants and fishers of Northmaven', 1726.

That its not unknouen to any of yow that the fishing trade is the principall means providence has ordaind for the suport of the paroch of Northmaven, without which ye could neither subsist your families nor pay the land rent and other publick burdens. And that a matter so absolutlie necessary and beneficiall should be carried on, improven and suported upon such a certain and reasonable footing as might most contribute for the good and advantage of the paroch in generall, without regaird to the privat intrest of any particulor person who may ather oppose the publick good or be uterlie incapable to contrabute any thing therunto, is what I am perswaded no good man will refuse. Yet it is evident to all of yow that alltho I have these severall years past been at vast charges and expence in keeping up and carrying on the said trade att the port of Hildsweek, furnishing the paroch with necessarys, receiving ther fish, herrings, butter and oyll at all seasons of the year, and paying as much therfor as ever they formerlie had, or is given in the cuntrie, and often suplying those that wer not capable to pay for it, wherby a considerable parte of my stock is sunk in the hands of a great many poore people in the paroch, who, notwithstanding, I most still support. Yet if ther was 20 small traders seting up in the paroch having ech of them but 2 or 3 barrels of salt and some watters and tobacco the fishers will sell ther fish to them befor me at that same price I give them, and even my oun tenents that stand bound by ther tacks under a failie to the contrary ar not ashamed to act such a knaveish and dishonest parte. And therfor it is uterly impossible for me any longer to suport under that great charge and expences I am at in keeping up the trade at the said port, and goeing the risque and hazerd of importing necessarys for the said paroch, upon such a precarious and unreasonable footing that every litle trader who is at no charge it all, and is noways capable to suply the paroch with what is absolutlie necessary for them, should get as many fish as I doe, who lyes at the whole, and besids all the butter and herring most be left to me to take upon, which I have losed yearlie these years past upwards of £150 sterling just on purpose to serve the paroch, and therfor most now have matters setled upon such a foundation as that I may be capable to suplye the place and suport the charge I most be at in so dooing, or I most give up the trade intierlie.

But having the benefit and prosperity of the paroch of Northmaven mor in viwe then any profit or advantage I propose by the trade, I am satisfyed to goe into the following agreement for preventing of further truble, and hindering the fraudulent practices of such people as ar ather inclined therunto or may be intised into the same. And as I have a naturall right and power to oblige my oun tenents to accept therof, so I hop it will appeer so faire and reasonable to all that no honest man in the paroch, who ather regairdeth his oun intrest or the publick good, will refuse the same. That is unto all the underwriten person[s] who goes into this agreement I promise and oblidgeth me and my successors to furnish them with all necessarys they shall need for carrying on the fishing at the ordanary prices in the cuntrie, to receive all ther whit fish at the booth of Hildsweek, all seasons of the year, and to pay the comon price they have allways got for them, and to receive from them yearlie at least thirtie last of herrings, and what mor I can convenientlie take at the rate of £thrie pounds Scots per barrell. And for encurgeing the whit fishers ther shall not one barrel of herring be taken from any man within the said paroch that is not a white fisher to me or hath some concern therin. And that non may be induced to leave the white fishing to follow the herring ther shall not a herring be received from any fisher in Northmaven befor the last of Jully, so as every man may have equall chance for the herring and no disturbance made in the white fishing. I shall allso receive all the butter as formerlie, and ther oyll all seasons of the year at ten shillings Scots per can, of what is mor then pays the superior debt, for which causes and on the other part the whole afternamed persons promiseth and oblidgeth themselves and ther successors in the roums and lands they now possess to deliver all the fish catched by them, with ther buter, oyll and herrings, at the booth of Hildsweek, unto the merchant ther for the time being, and whoever of the saids persons shall sell or dispose upon any ther saids goods to any person or persons, upon any pretence whatsomever, untill first making offer of them at the said booth of Hildsweek, and that they ar ther refused, shall forfite the sume of six pounds Scots mony for ech parcell of the saids goods so sold or disposed of, as penallty for breach of this agreement, which is to continue for the space of seven years, the first wherof being the year one thousand seven hundred and twintie seven years.

The above remonstrance being publickly read in open court befor James Cheyne of Tangwick, stewart substitute sitting in judgment, the following persons particularly called, viz. Hercules Jameson in Hagraster, Magnus Horrubson in Lunaster, Magnus Thomason in Sulem, George Anderson in Lunaster, John Robertson in Sulum, Malcom Donaldson in Clothester, James Donaldson ther, Hary Ollason in Burraland, Andrew Ollason in Orange, James Johnson in Gluss, Andrew Gilbertson ther, John Gilbertson ther, Laurence Gilbertson ther, Malcolm Gilbertson in Burgon, William Johnson in Gairdon of Gluss, John Grub in Gluss, Gilbert Robertson in Nistaseter, Andrew Porteus in Turvaster, Thomas Williamson in Fiblaster, Gilbert Pitcairn ther, George Nicolson in Eastweek, Thomas Mowat in Eastness, William Nicolson in Colloquoy, Alexander Robertson, Robert Broun in South Shade, Robert Robertson in Norwick, Thomas Williamson in Hogon, John Tulloch in Lien, Magnus Gilbertson in Quefirth, David Smith ther, Olla Nicolson [in] Crukseter, James Williamson in Voe, Andrew Robertson in Swinaster, John Williamson in Urafirth, Patrick Tulloch in Asseter, William Robertson ther, Hendrie Thomason in Helliar, Robert Haryson in Ocran, Patrick Lawrenson in Tingon, Hercules Philip ther, Andrew Philip ther, James Findlason, Magnus Gilbertson, James Gilbertson, Hary Haryson, James Ollason, Hary Ollason, Thomas Jameson, James Nicolson, John Nicolson, all in Hamnavoe, Hary Gilbertson in Muran, Olla Robertson in Brehouland, James Robertson, Arthur Robertson, both in Avensgarth, John Porteus in Bordigarth, John Jameson in Liascol, Nicol Johnson, James Johnson in Vinsgarth, John Mowat in Stow, John Gray in Stow, Gilbert Thomason in P[riest]houland, Donald Nicolson ther, Alexander Christopherson, Robert Johnson, both in Frangord, Thomas Reid ther, James Robertson in Breckon, William Mowat ther, Thomas Williamson in Gairdhouse, John Jameson in Gairdhouse, James Reid now in Stenness, Donald Williamson in Breweek, George Broun in Sandwick, Simon Broun, Robert Broun in Stovabreck, John Halcrow, James Halcrow, James Broun, John Clerk, Nicol Halcrow, John Anderson, George Broun senior, Hary Ollason, Olla Haryson, Peter Ollason, Andrew Ollason, John Manson, Alexander Clark, Andrew Smith, Simon Smith in Niddister, Thomas Ollason in Olnesfirth, Hary Williamson in Orbuster, Lawrence Thomason ther, Hary Haryson in Hammer, John Haryson, James Danielson ther, Thomas Henderson, Andrew Henderson in Enesfirth, Andrew Johnson ther, Lawrence Johnson, John Laurenson in Gunnaster, Andrew Williamson in Mangaster, Gilbert Cheyne in Ilsburgh, John Mowat of Skea. All unanimusly went in to the above agreement in all points therein contained.

In testimony whereof thir presents is signed at Hildsweek the nintenth day of October Jaj VIJc and twenty six years, in presence of the said judge by him, these underwriten witnesses and consenters thereto, upon this and the other side of this paper. James Cheyne, Thomas Gifford, James Oliphant, William Mackintosh. [*On verso*:] John Mowat, Donald Williamson, John Grub, David Gilbertson, George Niccollson, James Halcrow, James Broun, John Williamson, Andrew Smith, Gellbart Robartson, Andrew Portice, Robert Robertson.

Shetland Archives, D.6/131/2.

8. *Planking of Sooth Cunningsburgh, 1780.*

Measurement and division of South Cunningsburgh, February 1780, each plank containing sixteen hundred square fathoms

Planks	fathoms	p[lanks]	f[athoms]	p[lanks]	f[athoms]			merks
						VESTANORE AND CLIVAGARTH		
5	1072	...	...	...	...	Infields	or Vestanore	Computed 24
5	1589	...	...	...	...	Outfields	for 18 merks	ar 18 for
7	1120	...	...	...	...	Outfields in Clivagarth	and Clivagarth	Vestanore
----------		19	581			Grass in do.	for 6 merks	and 6 merks
		6	10			Grass in Vestanore		for Clivagarth
		40	800	...	...	Meadows in do.		
		5	500	...	...			
			----------	71	291			
						THE CLAPHOULL OR NORTH DIVISION		
10	874	...	...	...	...	Infields		
23	360	...	...	...	...	Outfields		
----------		33	1174					Computed 48
		21	640	...	...	Grass		
		6	88	...	...	Its proportion of 14 planks publick meadow		
			----------	61	302			
						THE BEOLKA OR LOWER PLANK		
18	874	...	...	...	...	Infields		
5	370	...	...	...	...	Outfields		
----------		23	1244					Computed 42
		13	730	...	...	Grass		
		5	478	...	...	Proportion of 14 p[lanks] meadows		
			----------	42	852			
						VOXTER AND OUT OF THE TOWN		
7	1500	...	...	...	...	Infields		
10	6	...	...	...	...	Outfields		
----------		17	1506					Computed 21
		19	357	...	...	Grass		
		2	1034	...	...	Proportion of 14 p[lanks] meadow		
			----------	39	1297			
						ANNESS		
2	-	...	...	...	...	Infields		
4	160	...	...	...	...	Outfields		
----------		6	160					Computed 9
		37	94	...	...	Grass		
			----------	43	254			
				257	1396			144

Vestanore of all kinds of corn land per merk, near $4/5$
Claphool of do. per do., near $3/4$
Beolka of do. per do. 2 p[lank] above $1/2$ of do. per do.
Voxter of do. per do. above $4/5$
Anness of do. per do. about $2/3$

Gross contents

	p[lanks]	fath[om]s		
Vestanore and Clivagarth	71	291	Computed	24 merks
Claphoul or north plank	61	302	do.	48
Beolka or south plank	42	852	do.	42
Voxter and out of the Town	39	1297	do.	21
Anness	43	254	do.	9
In all	257	1396	for	144 merks

Vestanore and Clivagarth seems to contain of gross contents near	3 planks of ground for every merk of land
Claphoull plank about	1½ plank per merk
Beolka do. about	1 plank per merk
Voxter and out of the Town near	2 plank per merk
Anness about	4½ plank per merk

Observations

1st. Vestanore is safe from sea gust, it has the hill or commonty almost round it, and the sea with plenty of ware at their doors. It has more than its proportion of meadow ground, and all its grass ground is improveable.

2d. Aness is much liable to sea gust, has little ware and is two miles from the hill or commonty; it has no meadows, and near the half of all its grass grounds is next to useless, and can neither be improved by grass or corn for want of soil.

3d. Claphoul has very improveable outfields, which probably can be extended and increased by lying next the hill dyke; it is near peats, truck and hill grass, and has plenty of improvable grass ground within dyke, while Aness, Voxter and Beolka can never be made larger, and are in a manner precluded from the hill or commonty, except with very great trouble, by being surounded by the sea and other planks, as will be seen by the plan.

4th. Voxter and Out of the Town. This plank consists of small ditatched spotes of tolerable corn ground, but all of it cannot be ploughed; it has tolerable good grass, but as above is far from the hill or commonty, and hardly a possibility of a road to the hill, even for peats.

5th. Beolka is mostly infields and good grass and meadows; it all lys very compact and is very easy laboured, but as above by being surounded by other planks and the sea, it can never be made larger, and being in the best state of cultivation it can never be made better, yet it is a little liable to sandblowing.

Anness, by its distance from the ware and the publick meadow, can enjoy no part of either, but every other plank and heritor can have the same interest in the ware, hill dykes, and privileges in the commonty that they had before. It must be observed that every plank must see to its own tounmails, and most all of them allow through them the usual publick, private, sea and hill roads, ware, midding steeths or beatches, and every other accustomed privilege, for all these things have been considered, and proper allowances made to each plank in the consultation at affixing the number of merks to each plank.

37 plank 1120 fathoms is the whole extent of corn grass and other grounds possessed by Sumburgh in outsets in South Cunningsburgh, for which all the other heritors possessing 26 merk in all will get a proportional share of new grounds without dykes set of to them, which proportion is 26/144 or six planks and 1294 fathoms.

The forgoing measurement of Cunningsburgh was made from the 3d to the 12th February 1780, by James Leisk, John Hutchison, John Leisk, Peter Tulloch of Scarpigarth, Laurence Leisk and Donald Bain, and also the forgoing computations of the number of merks allotted to each plank were made by them at the same time, to the exactness of which they are willing to give their oaths, as also to the number of merks alloted to each plank or division, they are willing to swear as to the best of their knowledge to be just and equitable, all advantages and disadvantages considered to the best of their knowledge, without the smallest favour or partiality to any person or plank. They likewise acknowledge every part of the above observations, especially these concerning the tounmails, roads and all necessary privileges hitherto in use amongst the 8 lasts to be just and reasonable. Lastly they hope it will be found that whatever disadvantages some planks or divisions may appear to labour under, they have made such planks sufficiently amends in justice, by discerning to them a fewer number of merks.

Given at Scarpigarth this fifteenth day of February 1780, and subscribed by us before these witnesses: Mr Arthur Nicolson junior of Lochend and James Forbes, clerk to John Bruce of Sumburgh. (Signed on the fourth and last pages thus:) James + Leisk his mark, John Hutchison, John Leisk, Patrick Tulloch, Lawrance Leask, Arthur Nicolson witness, James Forbes junior witness. (Follows what is wrote after signing the foregoing paper:) Nota. Donald Bain is at present absent, but has previously acknowledged to the plankers his willingness to sign the above.

Shetland Archives, SC.12/53/5, folio 74: 'Sundry views of the plankers of Cunningsburghs measurement and computation, 12th February 1780'.

9. *Four fishing tenure contracts, 1774-1839*
It is contracted and agreed betwixt Sir John Mitchell of Westshore, barronet, heritable proprietor of the lands after mentioned, on the one part, and Thomas Fordyce, tenant in Grutton, on the other part, in manner following, that is to say the said Sir John Mitchell has set, and by these presents setts and in tack and assedation letts to the said Thomas Fordyce, his heirs and executors (excluding all assignees or subtenants), all and whole my eight merks land in the island of Fetlar in the room of Aith, in Zetland, with the houses, biggings, yeards, outside, inside, mosses, meadows, muirs, common pasturage, shores, tang ebb, fishings, and that [for] the space of three years next and immediately following the said Thomas Fordyce his entry thereto, which is declared to have begun at the term of Martinmas last bypast, notwithstanding the date hereof, and from thence forth to endure during the space forsaid, freely, quietly, well and in peace, without revocation; which tack the said Sir John Mitchell binds himself, his heirs and successors to warrant to the said Thomas Fordyce and his forsaids, at all hands and against all deadly [*torn*] cause.

And on the other part the said Thomas Fordyce, by his acceptation hereof, binds and obliges himself, his heirs, executors and successors and intromittors with his goods and gear whatsomever, to make good and thankfull payment and delivery to the said Sir John Mitchell, his heirs and successors, or to their factors in their name, of the sum of six pounds eight shillings Scots money, as the money rent of the said lands, at the term of Martinmass, and that yearly dureing the currency of this tack, beginning in this current year for the crop of the same, and so forth yearly thereafter, dureing the other years of this tack; and further, the said Thomas Fordyce engageth himself and his forsaids, duiring the existance of this tack, to fitt out, on their own charges, the fourth share of a six oard boat to the haff for ling fishing, dureing the fishing or summer season each year, as other tenants in the country do, the said boat to have to the extent of betwixt thirty and fourty growndlines of sixty fathoms each, sufficiently provided with hooks and other fishing materialls; and it is agreed that the fishing, both cod and ling and tusk, shall be delivered unsplit to the said Sir John Mitchell and his foresaids at his booth in Funzie, or any other place within the island of Fetlar he shall appoint most convenient, as the said Thomas Fordyce hereby, for him and his foresaids, sells to the said Sir John Mitchell the whole ling, cod and tusk to be catched by him and partners dureing this tack, at the rate of four pence [sterling *interlined*], each ling of twenty seven inches, and all ling under that size to be made up in the usual methods of guilding fish according to the practice of this country; one penny sterling each tusk of fourteen inches and upward; one penny and half penny sterling each cod of eighteen inches and upwards. And the said Thomas Fordyce also sells to the said Sir John Mitchell and his foresaids his whole other product made by him on the said farm, such as cattle, oyl and others, the said Sir John Mitchell paying for each article thereof conform to the current price in the country for the time, upon payment or offer thereof, the said Sir John Mitchell be preferable to all other persons whatsoever; again the said Sir John Mitchell is to provide the said Thomas Fordyce in boats and other fishing materialls at the current price for the time, so as that the said Thomas Fordyce, for want of these materialls, shall not be hindered in prosecuting the fishing business; further, the said Thomas Fordyce obliges himself to pay the ordinary number of days labour of one man each day, with the cess or land tax and other publick burdens yearly, according to the practice of this country, and also to keep up the houses and dykes in good repairs, and to leave them and the land in the same condition at the end of this tack, without any warning or process in law to that effect, and both parties engageth to perform their respective parts of the premises to each other, under the penal sum of twenty four pound Scots money to be paid by the party failing to the other party besides performance.

In witness whereof these presents are written on this and the preceeding page by me James Smith in Funzie, factor for Sir John Mitchell, and signd by the said Sir John Mitchell, and the said Thomas Fordyce has affixed his usual mark hereto, because he cannot write, at Funzie the eleventh day of August Jaj VIJc and seventy four years, before these witnesses: James Smith, John Smith in Strand, John Jameson in Odseter, William Gauden of Averland.

Shetland Archives, D.7/71/23.

Lerwick 13th May 1806. Magnus Georgeson. In consequence of our communing respecting the outset of Hallbrake, presently laboured by you, lying in the parish of Aithsting in Shetland, I hereby engage and agree to set you said outset of [*blank*] upon the following conditions: for your encouragement you are to have it for seven years from Martinmas first, free of all rent; but upon the expiry of said seven years and from Martinmas eighteen hundred and thirteen you are to pay to me and my heirs the sum of twelve pounds Scots, four poultry fowls or two geese, all at Lerwick, besides rowing to the ling fishery in a six oar'd boat to me from this date and during the currency of your tack (if able and in health), for such sum of fee as I may yearly give to any other of my tenants; and failing of your rowing to the sea to me you are in that case hereby taken bound to pay me or my heirs yearly the sum of eighteen pounds Scots, with the poultry fowls or geese above mentioned. On these conditions only I hereby bind and oblige myself and heirs to continue you in said possession for all the days of your life, and to warrant the same to you at all hands, and further, should you be engaged or employed in the herring fishery, you are likewise taken bound to deliver them to me or to my order, on the same terms my other tenants deliver them upon. Hereby declaring that if you shall be found to dispose of any fish, herrings or oil past me, in that case, and on the fact being proven, this letter of tack shall become void and null and of none effect, or if during the currency of your tack you shall allow any part of your yearly rent to be due for three months after the annual term of payment, in that case it shall be in my option to declare this tack null and void, any law or practice to the contrary notwithstanding, declaring also that if at any time either party shall require the other to have this letter of tack extended on stampt paper, the same shall be immediately complyed with, and the expence thereof defrayed by both parties equally. Heartily wishing you success I am, Magnus, your well wisher. (signed) Andrew Grierson. To Magnus Georgeson, tenant on the outset in the parish of Aithsting.

Shetland Archives, SC.12/53/8, folio 94.

Lerwick 28 November 1811. Robert. I hereby make you certain of the half of Upperhoulland, being that half possessed by George Manson. The debt of which is twenty two pounds Scotts in money and one half lispound of butter, with four poultry fowls and 2 casies, you paying the scatt, with which I have no concern. The above is all the rent you pay yearly to me, providing you row to the sea to me, in which event you receive £16 Scotts in money of fee and 40d. per hundred ling the boat fishes you are placed in, as you have received this some years back. Or should you any year wish to go to Greenland, in that event you yearly pay me twenty shillings to enable me to fee a man in your room any year you do not row to me. These are my terms, which when you consider of let Mr Tulloch advise me of your agreeing to them, and I shall immediately send you out a missive tack for seven years duly signed by me, and for your putting your mark thereto. I am, Robert, your well wisher: Andrew Grierson. (addressed) to Robert Georgeson in Howster, Aithsting parish. Written by Peter Tulloch, residenter in Lerwick: Peter Tulloch.

Shetland Archives, SC.12/53/8, folio 103.

Minute of agreement between Sir A. Nicolson and his tenants in the island of Papa Stour.

Sir A. Nicolson agrees to set his lands at the same rent [as formerly *deleted*] viz. twelve shillings per merk, besides the public burdens &c., as formerly. He farther agrees to advance to the tenants fishing materials at prime cost and to contract with a merchant or merchants to receive the tenants produce, and to credit them for the same, deducting only a small commission for his trouble and risk. The tenants on the other hand engage faithfully to deliver their produce to such contractor at the rates agreed for by Sir A. Nicolson on their behalf, and that under a penalty of ten shillings whenever such agreement shall be contravened by them by their disposing of their produce to others than the contractor, the said penalty to be paid to the contractor and recovered by him. Tenants persisting in this practice will be warned and summarily removed from the property.

In witness whereof this minute of agreement is signed by Sir Arthur Nicolson and the tenants of Papa Stour. Grimasta May 6th 1839. Arthur Nicolson. N.b. The price of the produce will be put at once to each mans credit to the extent of his land rent and the charges upon him and any surplus beyond that will be paid to the tenant in cash as soon as Sir Arthur receives it from the contractor, but Sir Arthur is not to be responsible for such surplus till received by him. Grimasta May 6th 1839. Arthur Nicolson.

[*in pencil*: The tenants will sign here]

Thomas Fraser; Magnus Isbister; John Isbister; Thomas Georgeson; Abram Fraser; William Isbister; George Pole; Gabril Coutts; Joseph Isbister; Gideon Willimson;

Alexander Fraser; Robert Cout; Fraser Jameson; Magnus Jameson; Laurence Fraser; George Fraser; Thomas Fraser junior; John Sinclair; Laurence Sinclair; Arthur Twat; Peter Fraser; George Hay; Henry Twat; James Peterson; John Coutts; William Georgison.

Shetland Archives, D.24, box 69, item 5. All sign with a mark except Thomas Fraser, Magnus Isbister, John Isbister, Thomas Georgeson, Abram Fraser, William Isbister, Gabril Coutts, Fraser Jameson, John Coutts and William Georgison. The marks are usually witnessed by Gideon Henderson and Scott Robertson.

Index

A
Aachen 6
Adomnán, biographer 62
Aiklay, Thomas in Utrabister (1620s) 20n.
Aith
—, Bressay 84
—, Cunningsburgh 26
—, Fetlar 18n., 94
Aithsetter, Cunningsburgh 24n., 26
Alexander
— Christopherson in Frangord (1726) 91
— Robertson (1726) 91
Andersen, Per Sveaas, historian xi n.
Andrew
— Bartilsone, Basta (1667) 84-5
— Gilbertson in Gluss (1726) 91
— Henderson in Enesfirth (1726) 91
— Hendriesone, Brughe (1667) 84
— Johnsone (1667) 85
— — in Enesfirth (1726) 91
— Ollason (1726) 91
— — in Orange (1726) 91
— Robertson in Swinaster (1726) 91
— Williamson in Mangaster (1726) 91
Aness, Cunningsburgh 26, 27, 28, 92, 93
Antony Mansone, Nebeback (1667) 85
Aresdaill, Yell 87
Arnold Mansone, Nebeback (1667) 85
Arthur Robertson in Avensgarth (1726) 91
Avragarth *see* Evrigert

B
bailie 83
bailie courts xv, 44, 73, 73-4
Bain, Donald (1780) 93, 94
Balfour, William (1774)18n., 24n., 42, 45-6
Baliasta, Unst, scattald of 39
Ballantyne, John, researcher 61n., 70n.
Barnes, Michael, linguist 38n.
barrel *see also* peice
— xvi n., 19, 83, 84, 90
Basta Vo, Yell 86
beer xvi n., 19

Belaribs, Ure, Eshaness 89
Bell estate 50
Beneserge, Yell 86
Benigert, Nort Roe 38
Benson, Bruce 50
Beolka, Cunningsburgh 26, 27, 92, 93
bere xi
Bergen xi n., 10
Bibire, Paul, linguist 10n., 38n., 82
Biggins, Da, Papa Stour 8, 11, 12, 13, 18
Bigton, Dunrossness 4, 22, 23, 25
Biorg of Cullivoe (1307) xvi
Birsay, Orkney 21
bishopric estates 59, 68
Bjørkvik, Halvard, historian 39n.
Black Death xv, 5
Black estate 50
Blance
—, Jeannie (1930s) 20
—, Kirstie (1930s) 20
Blett, Cunningsburgh 46-7
Blosta, Cunningsburgh 26
Blunkett, David, politician 7
Bolt, Thomas (1809) 26n.
boltal 10
booth
—, fishing 69
—, of Funzie 94
—, of Hillswick 90
Bothwell, Adam, bishop of Orkney 60
Bowagardie, Yell 88
Bragister/Brekasætr, Papa Stour xv, 2, 3, 8, 9, 10, 11, 12, 13, 14, 16, 17, 18, 81
Brand, David, sheriff and commissioner 78
Brawick, Yell 85
Breadelds, Ure, Eshaness 89
Brebister, Waas 22-3
Breck, Bigton 22
Brekasætr *see* Bragister
Bremen 6
Bremer, Cunningsburgh 26
Brenner, Robert, historian 78, 80
Bressay 43, 59, 84
Brig of Waith, Orkney 60n.

Brind, Cunningsburgh 26
Brindister, Gulberwick 24n.
Broo, Dunrossness 4, 25
Broun
—, George in Sandwich (1726) 91
—, — senior (1726) 91
—, James, skipper (1657) 70n.
—, — (1726) 91
—, Robert in South Shade (1726) 91
—, — in Stovabreck (1726) 91
—, Simon (1726) 91
Brown, John, fishcurer 77
Bruce
—, Andrew of Muness 4n., 25
—, John (I) of Sumburgh 28, 46
—, — (II) of Sumburgh 29
—, —, junior of Sumburgh 49, 72
—, Laurence of Cultmalindie (1570s) 45
—, Scipio of Ure (1626) 83
—, William (1646) 40n.
—, — (1775) 23
—, — of Symbister (1797) 29
Brugh(e)
— scattald, Yell 85-6
—, Bressay 84
—, Yell 85
Brunsdeald, Ure, Eshaness 89
bu 9
bull (of oil) 83
Bulwer Lytton, Edward, novelist 63
Buness estate 50
Burgess, J.J. Haldane, poet 55
Burra 21, 77
Burrafirth, Unst 4, 50, 58-9, 60, 61
Burraness, Cunningsburgh 26, 27-8
Burravoe, North Roe 77
butter xv, xvi, xvii, 8, 19, 39, 66, 74, 76, 83, 84, 90, 96

C
Caldback, Delting 22n., 41, 60
Caldbackness, Delting 59
Calsta, Northmavine 38
Cameron, Major Thomas 49, 52
can (of oil) 83
Catfirth, Nesting 46
cattle 23, 38n., 41, 74, 94, 95
Channerwick, Dunrossness 24n., 44
Chaucer, Geoffrey, poet 19
Cheyne
—, Gilbert in Ilsburgh (1726) 91
—, James of Tangwick (1726) 91
—, Patrick of Valey (1632) 4n.
Cheyne estate 50

Claphoull, Cunningsburgh 26, 27, 92, 93
Clark, Alexander (1726) 91
Clerk, John (1726) 91
Clet, Whalsay 43
Cliff, Unst 50, 55-6, 59
Cliff Skerry, Burrafirth 59
Clivagarth, Cunningsburgh 26, 92
Cloden, Yell 87
Cloth *see* wadmal
—, linen xvi
Clouston, J. Storer, historian 14, 32n.
Cluness, Wilma 22n.
Collaquey, Northmavine 33
Cologne *see* mark, Cologne
Colt *see also* Cout, Coutts
—, Robert (163_) 23n.
Colvasetter, burn of, Yell 86
Commissioners of Supply 46
Cooper, Susan, local historian 48n.
Couper, George, fishcurer 66
corn xv, 8, 10, 11, 13, 17, 19, 28, 34, 35, 89, 93
corn barrel 8n.
corn stack 34, 35
cornteind 83
Coultisuek *see* Culswick
Country Acts 21, 44, 46
Cout *see also* Colt, Coutts
—, Robert in Papa Stour (1839) 97
Coutts *see also* Colt, Cout
—, Gabril in Papa Stour (1839) 96
—, John in Papa Stour (1839) 97
—, — 44n.
Crofters Commission (1889 etc.) 54, 55, 76, 78
Crofters Holdings (Scotland) Act xv, 54, 78
Cromertie, John (1626) 83
Crookster, Delting 41, 60
crown estates 63, 84
Culbensburcht, Bressay, 84
Culswick/Coultisuek, Sandsting 22, 23, 25, 38
Cunningsburgh
—, Nort 25, 26, 27, 28, 31
—, Sooth 25, 26, 27, 28, 50, 56, 92-4
Cups, The, Ure, Eshaness 89
currency, Shetland xv, xvi-xvii, 4, 5, 6, 8, 12, 16, 17, 18
cuttell (of cloth) 83, 84

D
Dale
—, Delting 4

Dale *continued*
—, Tingwall 50
—, Waas 33
Daniel Erasmussone, Arisdaill (1667) 85
Dasetter, Yell 86
Dedistoun, Mairtein (1605) 39
Deer Forest Commission (1894) 50, 56
Delting
— 49, 52, 60
—, North 50
Denmark
— 6
—, king of xv, 68
Donald
— Nicolson in Priesthouland (1726) 91
— Williamson in Breweek (1726) 91
Donaldsone, Peter (1667) 84
Douglas, Gavin, poet 62-3
Duisburg 6
Duncan, Gilbert, notary (1821) 88
Dyelda-gooe, Yell 85

E
Eallenadeald, Ure, Eshaness 89
Easter Great Gerdistrengs, Ure, Eshaness 89
Edmondston
—, Andrew of Hascosea (1667) 85
—, David Charles, landlord 49, 56
—, Laurence, doctor 72
—, Thomas, lexicographer 4n.
Eindrid, Sir (1299) 2, 9, 81
Eirik
— Ungi (1299) 81, 82
—, Sir (1299) 2, 9, 81
Elizabeth I, queen 19
Eners-gord, Yell 86
entry-fine 20n.
Erlend
— Alfeit (1299) 81, 82
— Geirmundson (1299) 81, 82
Eshaness 41-2
Evrigert/Avragarth, Papa Stour 8, 12, 13, 16, 17, 18
Exnaboe, Dunrossness 22n.
eyrir *see also* ounce
— xvi
Eystein, bishop of Oslo (1395) 14

F
Fair Isle 4, 33, 70
fat goods 19
fathom
— (of peats/dykes) 21, 22

—, square (of land) 27, 92, 93
Faugla-feyll, Yell 85
Fealsteake, Ure, Eshaness 89
Fedeland, Northmavine 74
Ferlies, The, Ure, Eshaness 89
Fetlar 17, 44, 48, 50, 55, 56, 94
Fiblister, Northmavine 54, 82
Findlason, James in Hamnavoe (1726) 91
Finzie *see* Funzie
fish, fisheries *see also* fishing tenure, stock fish
— xv, xvi n., xvii, 15, 19, 45, 46, 47, 48, 52, 54, 56, 58, 59, 60, 65-80, 89-91, 94-7
fishing tenure xiii, xv, 45, 46, 47, 48, 65-80, 94-7
Fitful Head, Dunrossness 47
Fladabister, Cunningsburgh 29, 31, 32
Flaws, James (1872) 66-7
Foote, Peter, linguist 38n.
Forbes
—, James, clerk (1780) 94
—, —, junior (1780) 94
Fordyce, Thomas in Grutton (1774) 94-5
Forrats, Da, Sandness 34
Foula 78
Framgord, Eshaness 42
Francis Johnsone, Awick (1667) 85
Fraser
—, Abram in Papa Stour (1839) 96
—, Alan, local historian 33
—, Alexander in Papa Stour (1839) 97
—, Andrew, North Setter (1667) 84
—, Christie 23n.
—, George in Papa Stour (1839) 97
—, James, Brughe (1667) 84
—, Laurence in Papa Stour (1839) 97
—, Mary 22n.
—, Peter in Papa Stour (1839) 97
—, Thomas in Papa Stour (1839) 96
—, —, junior, in Papa Stour (1839) 97
Frisia 19
Frustrenge, Ure, Eshaness 89
Fuglaskerrie, Eshaness 89
Funzie, Fetlar 18n., 29, 30, 33, 94, 95

G
Garderhouse, Eshaness 42
'Gardie'/'Garden' Papa Stour 3, 12, 16, 17, 18
Gardie, Unst 58
Gardon, Unst 42
Garth *see* Gert
Garth, The, Ure, Eshaness 89

Garth estate 50, 52
gate *see* grind
Gathrow Guttromesdoghter (1641) 58-9
Gauden, William of Averland (1780) 95
Gear, George, local historian 33
—, Wendy, local historian 48n.
George
— Anderson in Lunaster (1726) 91
— Nicolson in Eastweek (1726) 91
Georgeson
—, Magnus (1806) 95-6
—, Robert in Howster (1811) 96
—, Thomas in Papa Stour (1839) 96
—, William in Papa Stour (1839) 97
Germany, North xv, 68
Gert/Garth
—, Delting 41, 60
—, Dunrossness 8n., 50, 53
Gifford/Gifhart
—, Arthur of Busta 18n.
—, Janet (1632) 4n.
—, Mans (1626) 83
—, Thomas of Busta 16, 38, 46, 71, 72, 73, 75, 89-91
Gilbert
— Robertson in Nistaseter (1726) 91
— Thomason in Priesthouland (1726) 91
Gord, Cunningsburgh 26
Gordon, James, minister 75
Gotland 6
Goudie, Gilbert, historian 44, 55
Gramsci, Antonio 80
grass 27, 28, 30, 32-3, 40, 89, 92, 93
Graveland scattald, Yell 88
Gray, John in Stow (1726) 91
Great Custahoulls, Ure, Eshaness 89
Greenland 48, 96
Gregorius Benedictson (1299) 81, 82
Gremesta *see also* Grimasta
—, Yell 88
Grierson
—, Andrew of Quendale (1870s) 53, 72
—, — (1806) 95-6
Grimasta *see also* Gremesta
—, near Lerwick 96
grind/gate 35, 43
Grindascoll/Gryndescholl, Bressay 38
Groath, Ure, Eshaness 89
Grub, John in Gluss (1726) 91
Grunnavoe, Waas 35
Gryndescholl *see* Grindascoll
Guddateake, Ure, Eshaness 89
gudling *see* gullioun
Gudsher, Yell 85

gullioun/gudling/gylden xvi-xvii, 20n., 45, 82
Gunni of Gnipum (1299) 81, 82
Gunyelsta, Bressay 84
Guthrie, William, sheriff and commissioner 76-7, 78, 80
Gutrom
— Lowrancesone (before 1607) xvii
— Petersone (1641) 58
Guttald, Whalsay 38n.
gylden *see* gullioun

H
hagrie 41, 43-44
Håkon Magnusson, duke (later king) xv, 1, 9, 10, 14, 81, 82
Halcrow
—, Edward, Fladabister (1797) 29
—, James (1726) 91
—, John (1726) 91
—, Laurence, Fladabister (1797) 29
—, (1820s) 44
—, Malcolm, Fladabister (1797) 29
—, Nicol (1726) 91
—, William, Fladabister (1797) 29
Halfdan of Breuster (1299) 81
Hallbrake, Aithsting 95
Hallinkine, Ure, Eshaness 89
Halsten Olasone 59
Ham, Bressay 38
Hamburg-Bremen, archbishopric of 6n.
Hamneseter, Whalsay 43
Hanlon, Jo 31n.
Hans Sigurdsson (1490) 61
Hansa, Hanseatic cities 6, 68
Hansen, Lars Ivar, historian 9n.
Harald
— Fairhair, king of Norway xi, xii, 39
— in Burrafirth (1299) 81
Harper, John (1894) 40
Hary
— Gilbertson in Muran (1726) 91
— Haryson in Hammer (1726) 91
— — in Hamnavoe (1726) 91
— Ollason in Burraland (1726) 91
— — in Hamnavoe (1726) 91
— — of Seitter (1624) 22n.
— — (1726) 91
— Williamson in Orbuster (1726) 91
Hasund, Sigvald, historian xiii, 9n.
Hävernick, Walter, historian 6n.
Hawick, Daniell, South-Ledie (1667) 85
Hay
—, George in Papa Stour (1839) 97

Hay *continued*
—, James, merchant 72
Hay & Co. 66, 72, 79
Hayfield estate 50
hay, haystacks 27, 34, 35
Heddell, Mr (1797) 29
Heilla, Yell 85
Helle, Knut, historian 10
Hellono-whida, Yell 88
Henderson
—, Brucie, storyteller 60
—, Gideon in Papa Stour (1839) 97
—, Tom, antiquary 33
—, William of Gardie (1707) 71
—, —, portioner of Gloup (1667) 84
—, —, Funzie (1820s) 30
Hendrie Thomason in Helliar (1726) 91
Henry III, emperor of Germany 6n.
Henry
—, John, Papa Stour (1847) 18
—, William (1847) 18
Hercules Jameson in Hagraster (1726) 91
heritable jurisdictions, abolition of xiii, xv, 44
Herra, Da, Yell xvii
Hewgone, Bressay 84
Hibbert, Samuel 66
Hillswick, Northmavine 69, 90
hill dyke xi, 22, 32, 38, 41, 42, 43, 85, 87, 93, 95
hogaleave 42
Hollmennis-hogga, Yell 88
Holmsen, Andreas, historian xiii, 10
Holsagarth, Yell 88
Horsey, Jerom, traveller 19
Houlland scattald, Yell 85
Houlna-houl, Yell 85
Hoversta, Bressay 84
Howlls, Ure, Eshaness 89
Hoxsetter *see* Huxter
Hughson, James of Westsandwick (1792) 75
Hurdiback, Papa Stour 12, 13, 16, 17, 18
Hutchison
—, Freda 31
—, John, planker (1780) 94
—, Thomas of Creediknowe (1889) 76
Huxter/Hoxsetter, loch of, Whalsay 43

I
Iceland 60
Imsen, Steinar, historian xiii
infield 25, 27, 30, 92, 93
Innes, Cosmo, historian 1

Iona 62
Irvine
—, Thomas of Midbrake 22n., 40, 88
—, William (1872) 79-80
Irving, Robert, Seatter (1667) 85
Isbister
—, John in Papa Stour (1839) 96
—, Joseph in Papa Stour (1839) 96
—, Magnus in Papa Stour (1839) 96
—, William in Papa Stour (1839) 96
Ivar
— Sperra (1299) 81, 82
—, 'bondi' of Aith (1299) 81

J
Jakobsen, Jakob, lexicographer 32, 40n., 60
James
— Danielson (1726) 91
— Donaldson in Clothester (1726) 91
— Gilbertson in Hamnavoe (1726) 91
— Johnson in Gluss (1726) 91
— — in Vinsgarth (1726) 91
— Nicolson in Hamnavoe (1726) 91
— Ollason in Hamnavoe (1726) 91
— Robertson in Avensgarth (1726) 91
— — in Breckon (1726) 91
— Williamson in Voe (1726) 91
— in Swaresetter (1600) 21
Jam(i)eson
—, Fraser in Papa Stour (1839) 97
—, John in Odseter (1780) 95
—, — 38n.
—, Laurence, Channerwick (1829) 44
—, Magnus in Papa Stour (1839) 97
Jeromson, John 32
John
— Anderson (1726) 91
— Gilbertson in Gluss (1726) 91
— Haryson (1726) 91
— Jameson in Gairdhouse (1726) 91
— — in Liascol (1726) 91
— Laurenson in Gunnaster (1726) 91
— Manson in Culswick (1640) 22n.
— — (1726) 91
— Neveback (1600) 21
— Nicolson in Hamnavoe (1726) 91
— Petersone, Coppasetter (1667) 85
— Robertson in Sulum (1726) 91
— Williamson in Urafirth (1726) 91
Johnston, Alfred W., historian 40
Judas 2, 14, 81

K
kail-yard xi, 34
Keldabuster, Bressay 84
Keoda, Cunningsburgh 26
Kerevan, George 80
Kews, Unst, scattald of 39
Kininga-loighe, Yell 85
Kingsley, Charles, novelist 63
Kirk Strengs, Ure, Eshaness 89
Kirkabister, Bressay 38, 84
Knychtsone, Thomas (1593) 59, 84

L
Lamba-hifda, Yell 87
Lambhoga, Fetlar 50
landmeallis/land-rent/landskyld *see* rent
Lang, Andrew, man of letters 19
last
— (of goods or rent) 4, 5, 9, 12, 16, 17, 18, 19, 20, 90
— (of land) xiii, xv, 3-5, 7, 9, 11, 12, 13, 14, 15, 16, 17, 18, 19-31, 83, 84, 93
Laurence
— Garthsone, Nether Houll (1667) 85
— Gilbertson (1726) 91
— Johnson (1726) 91
— Thomason in Orbuster (1726) 91
Laurenson, Arthur, merchant and antiquary 55
Lawsdeald, Ure, Eshaness 89
leanger (tax) 83, 84
Leask/Leisk
—, James, planker (1780) 93, 94
—, Lawrence, planker (1780) 93, 94
—, Margaret (1626) 22n.
—, Robert, local historian 33
leidang 10, 39
leispund *see* lispund
Lerwick 72, 78, 95, 96
Leveneep, Lunnasting 34
Lewesetter, Whalsay 43
ley (unworked) land 40, 72, 89
Liascoll, Ure, Eshaness 89
Liascolldeald, Ure, Eshaness 89
lispund/leispund xvii, 8n., 83, 84
Litell
— Cussahowll, Ure, Eshaness 89
— Gerdistrengs, Ure, Eshaness 89
Littlaland, Fetlar 18n.
Low, George, traveller 75
Lübeck 6
Lunden, Kåre, historian xvi
Lunnasting 50

M
MacCulloch, John, chemist 79-80
Macgregor, Lindsay 17n.
Maclean, Calum, folklorist 60
Mae-da dales-woe, Yell 87
mæle/meil 3, 5n., 7, 8, 11, 13, 17, 81, 82, 83, 84
Magnus
— Daile (1602) 42
— Gilbertson in Hamnavoe (1726) 91
— — in Quefirth (1726) 91
— Henderson of Gardie (1641) 59
— Hognason (1299) 81, 82
— Horrubson in Lunaster (1726) 91
— Lagabøter, king 8, 9
— Mansone, Gloup (1667) 84
— Mathewsone, Ulsta (1667) 85
— Ollavesone (1667) 84
— Thomason in Sulem (1726) 91
Magnus Lagabøter's Landlaw 8, 62, 67
Mail, Cunningsburgh 26
Maimateake, Ure, Eshaness 89
Malcolm
— Donaldson in Clothester (1726) 91
— Gilbertson in Burgon (1726) 91
Malcolmson, Keetie 33
Mann, Andrina 33
Mans Robertsone in Hougoland (1626) 83
Manson
—, George (1811) 96
—, Jane, local historian 48n.
Margaret Halstensdoghter (1641) 58-9
mark/merk
— forngild 9n.
— of land xi, xv, xvi, xvii, 3, 4, 5, 7, 8, 9, 11, 12, 13, 14, 16, 17, 18, 20, 21, 22, 23, 24n., 25n., 26n., 27, 28, 29, 34, 35, 40, 53, 58, 59, 60, 61n., 76, 81, 82, 83, 84, 89, 92, 93, 94
—, burnt xi n., xvi, xvii n., 2, 7, 9n., 11, 81, 82
—, Cologne xv, xvi, 6
marks, various European 6
Marka, Yell 85
markebol 9, 14
Markina-gooe, Yell 87
Markins Houle, Yell 85
Marwick, Hugh, philologist xi, xii, xiii, 60n.
meadow 27, 28, 30, 40, 89, 92, 93
meil *see* mæle
Melbie, Sandness 4n., 22n.
Merkeiesmoode, Yell 85
Merkies-gooe, Yell 88

Mews/Mewhous
—, Bigton 22
—, Quarff 35
Mid Setter, Papa Stour 12, 13, 16, 17, 18
Mill-goe, Yell 85
Mitchell
—, James of Girlsta (1707) 71
—, Sir John of Westshore (1774) 94-5
—, Lady (1743) 74
Moar, Agnes (1894) 40
Moe-feyll, Yell 87
Montrose, Marquis of 21
Moore, Stewart 56n.
Morton, earl of 21
Mossa-houle, Yell 85
Mouat
—, Andrew of Hogaland 59, 60, 61
—, Gilbert (1624) 16n.
—, Hector (1698) 16
—, James (1698) 16
—, — (1709) 3n.
—, — (1723) 61
—, John in Stow (1726) 91
—, — of Skea (1726) 91
—, Patrick of Hamnavoe, yr 3n., 4n., 16n.
—, — of Ballwhally 16n.
—, Robert (1709) 3n.
—, Thomas in Eastness (1726) 91
—, William in Breckon (1726) 91
—, — (1761) 75-6
Mousa 46
Mowat *see* Mouat
Muckle Skerry 61
Muerastrengs, Ure, Eshaness 89
Murray, David of Clairden (1670s) 61

N
Nakken, Afhild, archivist 58n.
Napier Commission xi, 37, 54, 78
Napier, Lord 39, 40n., 47, 54, 78
Napoleonic wars xv, 72
Neathaburn, Quarff 35
Nebeback scattald, Yell 87
Neven
—, Gilbert, bailie of Yell 88
—, Ninian of Windhouse (1620s) 20n.
—, Robert of Windhouse (1761) 75-6
Nicol Johnson (1726) 91
Nicolson, Arthur of Bullister (1723)16n., 61, 71
—, —, junior, of Lochend (1780) 28, 94
—, Sir Arthur of Lochend 18, 31, 48, 96
Nicolson estate 50
Nightingale, Pamela, historian 6n.

Ninian Hendersone of Gardie (1667) 84
Nisbeit
—, Gilbert (1600) 21
—, James, Kunningsetter (1667) 84
—, Peter (1600) 21
—, —, Sellofirth (1667) 84
Nissetter, Northmavine 54
Norby, Sandness 32
Northhouse, Ure, Eshaness 89
Northoose, Papa Stour 3, 12, 13, 16
Norway xii, xvi, 2, 3, 5, 6, 9, 10, 14, 39, 40, 61, 67, 68, 81
Noss 61, 84
Nossound 84
Noube, Yell 88

O
oats xi, 89
oil 8, 19, 63, 66, 74, 84
Oliphant, James (1688) 89
Olla
— Haryson (1726) 91
— Nicolson in Crukseter (1726) 91
— Robertson in Brehouland (1726) 91
Olligert, Papa Stour 8, 12, 13, 16, 17, 18
ootset *see* outset
Opplands, Norway 9n.
Ordale, Unst 50
Orkney xi, xii, xiii, xv, 5, 6, 7, 8, 9, 14, 32, 37, 40, 45n., 59, 60n.
Osea Johnsone (1667) 85
Otterswick scattald, Yell 87
ounce *see also* eyrir
— xi, 5, 6
ounceland/uresland *see also* tirunga, uncia, unciate
— xi, xii, xv, 5, 6, 8, 9, 11, 13, 14
Outer Skaw, Unst 46
outfield 25, 30, 92, 93
'Out of the Town', Cunningsburgh 26
outset 46, 93, 95, 96
Øye, Ingvild, historian 2n.

P
'packit guidis' 83
pak (of cloth) 83, 84
Papa Stour xv, 1-18, 22, 25, 31, 34, 39, 45, 60, 61, 81, 82, 96-7
Papal scattald, Yell 38
Patrick Lawrenson in Tingon (1726) 91
peasant bondage xiii, 65, 66, 68, 78, 80
peat 21, 28, 34, 41, 42, 44, 46, 93
peice (barrel) 83
penny, Shetland and Orkney xi, xv, xvi,

xvii, 4, 5, 6, 8, 12, 16, 17, 18, 20, 26, 39, 82, 83, 84, 89
pennyland xi, xii, xv, 1, 2, 5, 6, 7, 8, 9, 11, 13, 14, 37, 81, 82
pennyworth 74
Perry, Jennifer 40n.
Peter Ollason (1726) 91
Peterson
—, George P.S., folklorist 10
—, James in Papa Stour (1839) 97
Philip
—, Andrew in Tingon (1726) 91
—, Hercules in Tingon (1726) 91
Pitcairn, Gilbert in Fiblaster (1726) 91
plank 25, 26, 27, 28, 92-4
planking 25, 26, 28, 31, 92-4
Plummer, Mary 49
Pole, George in Papa Stour (1839) 96
Pole, Hoseason & Co. 77
ponies 54
population increase/decrease xv, 15, 26, 29, 31, 40, 46, 52, 56, 69, 74
Porteus
—, Andrew in Turvaster (1726) 91
—, John in Bordigarth (1726) 91
potato xi, 35
Poulsen, Jóhan Hendrik W., linguist 38n.
poultry 95, 96

Q

Quendale estate 50
Quoyon, Yell 87
Quyes, The, Ure, Eshaness 89

R

raga 41
Raga, Yell 88
Ragnhild Simunsdatter xv, 1, 2, 3, 5, 8, 9, 10, 14, 81-82
Rampini, Charles, sheriff xi
Reafirth
— scattald, Yell 86, 87
— voe, Yell 86
Reid
—, James Stenness (1726) 91
—, Thomas in Frangord (1726) 91
Reirweik, Dunrossness 18n.
reki 62n.
Renfrew, Colin, prehistorian 45n.
rent/landmeillis/land-rent/landskyld xi, xv, xvii, 2, 3, 4, 5, 7, 8, 9, 10, 11, 12, 13, 14, 15, 16, 17, 18, 20, 26, 30, 39, 40, 45, 52, 54, 56, 65-80, 81, 82, 84
Renwanz, Marsha, anthropologist 56

Rhind, Bill, headmaster 7
Rich, Barnaby (1581) 19
rig aboot/rigga-rendal *see* runrig
Robert
— Haryson in Ocran (1726) 91
— Johnson in Frangord (1726) 91
— Petersone, Hamnavo (1667) 85
— Robertson in Norwick (1726) 91
Robertson
—, Gilbert, tailor (1626) 83
—, Scott (1839) 97
Roerdealds, Ure, Eshaness 89
Rue, Unst 50
runrig/rig aboot/rigga-rendal xi, xii, xv, 18, 24, 29-31, 32-3

S

St Ninians Isle 23
sáld (of corn) 3, 7, 8, 10, 11, 81, 82
Samuel, Raphael, historian xiii
Sand, Sandsting 63
sand-blowing 25, 27, 93
Sandison, Alexander, merchant 52
Sandnes, Jørn, historian 9n.
Sandness 4, 32, 33, 34
Sands, Patrick notary (1626) 83
Sandwick 21-2, 44
— scattald, Yell 85, 86, 87, 88
—, Whalsay 43
—, Yell 86
Saxby, Jessie M.E., author 40, 56
Scaitishous *see* Scatshoose
Scalloway Castle 21
Scarva-tonga, Yell 88
scat(t)/skat(t) 37, 38, 38, 39, 40, 41, 42, 45, 59, 83, 84, 96
scatland *see* scattald
scatlands 68
Scatness, Dunrossness 25, 25n., 26n.
Scatshoose, Bigton 4n., 22
scattald/scatland/scat-paying district xi, xiii, xv, 37-57, 84
Scots money xvii, 5, 6, 21, 70, 83, 90, 91, 94, 95, 96
Scott
—, James C., historian 75
—, Osie (1600) 21
—, — (1667) 85
—, Sir Walter, novelist 47, 63
seals 59, 60, 61, 62
Seatter *see* Setter
seaweed/tang/ware 28, 41, 62n., 93, 94
Selchiskerry 61
Sellafirth, Yell 85

Set(t)er/Seatter
—, Bressay, 84
—, Papa Stour 11n., 12, 13, 16, 17, 18
—, South Yell 87
—, Waas 22n.
—, Warth of, Yell 87
—, Whalsay 43
—, Yell 86
setting 5n.
share-cropping 65, 67, 68, 70, 71, 75, 80
sheep, sheep-farm 23, 31, 35, 40, 46, 48, 49, 50, 52, 54, 56
shilling, Shetland xv, xvi, 4, 5, 6, 26, 83, 84
Siglara-vatten, Yell 86
Sigurd, archdeacon (1299) 2, 9, 10, 81
Siladisks, Ure, Eshaness 89
Sinclair
—, Ann 33
—, George (1884) 37
—, Henry, Lord 7n.
—, Hugh of Brough (1670s) 61
—, James of Goit (1624) 4n.
—, — of Quendell (1632) 22n.
—, John of Gossabrugh (1667) 85
—, — in Papa Stour (1839) 97
—, Laurence of Broo (1630s) 25
—, — of Brough (1657) 70n.
—, — of Goit (1632) 22n.
—, — in Papa Stour (1839) 97
—, — of Quendale (1695) 70
—, Margaret (1661) 11n.
—, Robert of Quoyin (1626) 82-3
Sinsthoose, Bigton 22
sixern/six oared boat 66, 69, 74, 94
Skelberry, Dunrossness 46
Skene, W.F., historian xii n.
Skerries 61, 77
Skoeteake, Ure, Eshaness 89
Smith
—, Adam, economist 65, 67, 73, 79
—, Andrew (1726) 91
—, Cissie 24n.
—, David in Quefirth (1726) 91
—, Hance, historian 54, 71, 72
—, James in Funzie (1774) 95
—, John in Strand (1780) 95
—, Richard, historian 65n.
—, Simon in Niddister (1726) 91
Smyth, Andro (1628) 83
Snabrough, Unst 42
Soldian(s) 8n.
Soverlies, Ure, Eshaness 89
Spence & Co., merchants, Unst 52

Spence/Spens
—, Catherine 58
—, David, Houlland (1667) 84
—, James, Midbreck (1667) 84
—, —, Turfhous (1667) 84
—, John (1883) 39
—, — (1914) 31
—, William (1600) 21
Spufford, Peter, historian 6-7
Stenswall, Weisdale
—scattald of 39
sterling xi n., 5, 6, 90, 94, 95
Stewart
—, John (1624) 4n.
—, — (1626) 22n.
—, — Bruce of Symbister (1775) 23
—, Patrick, earl of Orkney 18n., 21, 42, 58, 59, 61, 62, 84
—, Lord Robert (1572) 60
—, William (1872) 73, 80
Stickle, Fredman (1818) 44
Stiflour, Yell 20n.
stock fish xvii
Strand scattald, Yell 87-8
Strand, Fetlar 18n., 46
Stromfirth, Weisdale 46
Sturascord, Yell 87
Sudderhoose, Papa Stour 3, 12, 13, 16
Sumburgh estate 50
Susastreng, Ure, Eshaness 89
Svein the priest (1299) 81
Sverre, king of Norway xv
Sweden 6
Symbister
— estate 50, 73
—, Whalsay 43, 66, 76

T
Tait, Ian 38n.
—, Jacob (1738) 40
tang *see* seaweed
Thomas
— Henderson (1726) 91
— Jameson in Hamnavoe (1726) 91
— Mathewsone, Coppasetter (1667) 85
— Ollason in Olnesfirth (1726) 91
— Williamson in Fiblaster (1726) 91
— — in Gairdhouse (1726) 91
— — in Hogon (1726) 91
Thomas, F.W.L., historian xi, xii, 5, 37, 40
Thomson, Willie, historian 8n., 14, 31, 33
Thorfinn Sigurdsson, earl of Orkney 6n.
Thorkell in Nes (1299) 2, 9, 10, 81
Þorsteinn Vilhjálmsson 37

Thorvald Thoresson xv, xvi, 1, 2, 5, 9, 10, 14, 81-2
Tingon, Northmavine 50
Tingwall xvii, 40, 48, 50
tinmel 32-3
Tipta Skerry, Unst 59
tirunga xii
toonmels/town-maills xi, 32-3, 93
Toun, Fetlar 44
town-maills *see* toonmels
Tresta
—, Aithsting 20n.
—, Fetlar 44
truck, truck-shops 67, 76, 77, 78, 79
Truck Commission (1871, 1872) 49, 73, 77
Trullakeldaes-houle, Yell 86
Tulloch
—, Andro (1626) 83
—, John in Cauldback 22n.
—, — of Fiblister (1626) xvii, 82-3
—, — in Lien (1726) 91
—, Patrick in Asseter (1726) 91
—, —, planker (1780) 94
—, Peter in Lerwick (1811) 96
—, Thomas of Feblesetter (before 1626) 82
—, Tom, folklorist 32
Tumblin, Sandsting 41
Tuptalands, Ure, Eshaness 89
Tupton, Unst 58
Turnbull, John (1841) 44n.
Tustian Turkelsone 58
Twat
—, Arthur in Papa Stour (1839) 97
—, Henry in Papa Stour (1839) 97
Twatt scattald, Aithsting 38
Tyrie, Laurence of Quoyon (1667) 85

U
Udhoose, Delting 20
Ulsta scattald, Yell 87
Umphray, Patrick of Sand (1641) 22n.
uncia xii
unciate xii
Union, Act of (1707) 70
Unna-Stakaes-Houla, Yell 87
Unst 17, 33, 39, 41, 44, 50, 52, 55-6, 59
Uphoose, Papa Stour 3, 4, 12, 13, 16
Upperhoulland, Aithsting 96
Upswall, Quarff 35
ure of land 28, 83, 84
Ure, Eshaness 24n., 89
uresland *see* ounceland

Uthascoll, Papa Stour 4, 16
Uyeasound, Unst 40

V
Vadament Stack, Woodwick, Unst 60
Vadsgarth, Cunningsburgh 26
Vaila 61
Vandringa-Vatten, Yell 87
Vee Skerries 60-1
Veeda Stack, Huxter, Whalsay 60
Veensgarth, Tingwall 50
Velzie, Fetlar 44
Vesker, Birsay, Orkney 60n.
Vesquoy, Waas 23
Vestagarth, Broo 4n.
Vestanore, Cunningsburgh 26, 28, 92, 93
Vesta Skerry, Burrafirth 59
Viga-dales-wo, Yell 87
Vinogradoff, Paul, historian 24, 26-7
Virdifield, Dunrossness 50
Voxter, Cunningsburgh 26, 27, 28, 92, 93

W
Wadbister, Bressay 43
Wadill Ayre, Burravoe, North Roe 77
wadmal/wodmell *see also* cloth, linen
— xv, xvi, xvi., 8, 39, 84
waif 62-3
waith, waithing 41, 58-63
Walker, John, sheep farmer 48-9, 52, 55
Wallace, William, patriot 60
Walster, Tingwall 40
Walterson
—, Aggie 32, 33
—, Gordon 32, 33
ware *see* seaweed
Waster Great Gerdistrengs, Ure, Eshaness 89
Weisdale 48, 50
Wester Quarff 35
West Holm, Burrafirth 59
Westing, Unst 60
Westsandwick
— scattald, Yell 88
—, Yell 88
whales 41, 63
whaling, Greenland 48, 96
Whalsay 50, 59, 76
Wickham, Chris, historian xiii n.
William
— Johnson in Gairdon of Gluss (1726) 91
— Manson (1603) 58, 59
— Nicolson in Colloquoy (1726) 91
— Robertson in Asseter (1726) 91

Williams, Gareth, historian xii n., 6n.
Williamsetter, Bigton 31
Williamson
—, George, Fladabister (1797) 29
—, Gideon in Papa Stour (1839) 96
—, James, Fladabister (1797) 29
—, Laurence, crofter-scholar 55
Windhouse
— scattald, Yell 86-7
—, Yell 50
Wischard, Sara 23n.

Witthöft, Harald, historian 6n.
wodmell *see* wadmal
Wood, Captain Robert (1651) 4n.
Woodwick, Unst 60

Y
Yell
— xvii, 21, 49, 52, 59, 62, 84-8
—, Mid 50
—, Nort 32, 50
Youngson, A.J., historian 65